BIBLE BASICS YOUTH ELECTIVES

The Joy of Sweat

Paul Woods, Editor

David C. Cook Publishing Co.
Elgin, Illinois—Weston, Ontario

This youth elective was developed through the combined efforts and resources of a number of David C. Cook's dedicated lesson writers. It was compiled and edited by Paul Woods and designed by Christopher Patchel and Jean Warfel, with cover design by Russ Peterson. Cover photo by Bakstad Photographics.

SERVICE
The Joy of Sweat

Scripture quotations are from the Holy Bible: New International Version (NIV), © 1973, 1978, 1984 by the New York International Bible Society. Used by permission of Zondervan Bible Publishers.

Published by David C. Cook Publishing Co.
850 N. Grove Ave., Elgin, IL 60120
Cable address: DCCOOK
Printed in U.S.A.

ISBN: 1-55513-875-6

CONTENTS

SERVICE: THE JOY OF SWEAT

Service isn't just a "religious" word. After all, who hasn't heard of full-service, mini-service, and self-service gas stations? How about drive-through service at the bank and the fast-food restaurant? Or express service in the checkout lane at the grocery store? We also see overnight service, emergency service, 24-hour service, speedy service, service with a smile, and more. Those of us who are old enough will even remember curb service. But what does *service* really mean?

For the Christian, service isn't just "giving the public what it wants." It isn't just doing a job, or whistling while you work, or even "finding a need and filling it." For the Christian, to *serve* is to be a *servant*.

Few people are lining up these days to apply for the position of servant. But for the Christian, servanthood is to become a life-style. Even harder to swallow is the fact that our service is to bring glory to God, not to us.

Kids and adults alike need to see that God intends that we serve Him, our fellow believers, and the world around us. This course can help get that message through to your teens.

As you lead this course, you'll have the opportunity to model servanthood to your kids. They need to see in you the example that Christ's disciples saw in Him. They need to understand that serving others is not just an admirable ideal to work toward, but a real, attainable way of life.

You'll begin this course by leading your kids through a section on service for God—responding to His call and following His commands. Next, you'll look at what it means to serve fellow believers. The last several sessions cover our service to the world—telling others about our Lord and showing them His love through our lives.

Your studies in this course won't end with mere information. Every session looks at Bible truths and applies them to the situations kids face. This course will challenge your kids to take action on their faith and to actively serve the God who has done so much for them.

Talking about faith is far easier than putting it into action. Sometimes service means hard, sweaty work. Sometimes it means speaking up in a threatening situation, or sacrificing an ambition or advantage in order to help others. But in seeking a life-style of service, you and your kids will be seeking to put God first.

Will you see the results of your service in this life? Will you be honored as a great philanthropist or model Christian? Perhaps not. But a better reward awaits: the "Well done, good and faithful servant," of the One we serve.

About the Bible Basics Youth Electives Series

Young people need firm foundations. Social events, games, and opinion-sharing discussions, good as they are, can't replace solid Bible learning. Whether that learning takes place in Sunday School, an evening Bible study, or another setting, it *must* be Bible-based and Christ-centered in order to give kids the timeless answers they need.

That's where Bible Basics Youth Electives come in. These 13-session courses allow your teens to spend time studying vital Scriptural truths *in depth.* The session plans provide you with background, questions and answers, and life response suggestions that will help you lead productive learning times.

Clear goals are stated for each three-step session, along with key verses and a list of the few items you'll need. You'll rarely need more than Bibles, pencils, paper, a chalkboard or flip chart, and copies of the reproducible student Action Sheets in the back of this book. There are no student manuals to buy; just make enough copies of the Action Sheets for your students and visitors.

You'll find the sessions easy to follow. Instructions to the leader are in regular type; things you might say directly to students are in bold type. Plenty of material for 45-60 minute sessions is included; feel free to adapt the plans to fit your time and group.

May God use His Word to build firm foundations in the lives of your young people—and to strengthen your own as well.

FAITHFUL SERVANTS

SESSION 1   **7**

Session Aim

That your students will develop their potential to be used by God as they discover and exercise previously unused abilities.

Key Verse

"Each one should use whatever gift he has received to serve others, faithfully administering God's grace in its various forms" (I Peter 4:10).

Things You'll Need

- Bibles
- Pencils
- "Lazy Sylvester" (Action Sheet 1A)
- "The Talent Tale" (Action Sheet 1B)
- Chalkboard and chalk
- Paper
- Tape
- Envelopes

***Who is the most talented person you know?** Who is the most talented person you know about? You may have thought of a musician, a writer, an athlete, or a business person. Most likely you thought of someone who is very successful in his or her field. And that person probably is very talented.*

But does that mean other people are totally untalented? Of course not—though many kids today think that way. Because they are not as talented as their favorite musician, actress, or athlete, some kids don't think they're talented at all.

This session points out that all of us are given abilities and talents by God. No one is left out. And God expects us to use the talents He gives us for His glory. Use this session to help your kids discover their own talents and to begin using those talents in service.

1 PULLING THE LOAD

Goal: That your kids will begin to see the importance of using talents they have.

As you begin today's session, pass out copies of "Lazy Sylvester" (Action Sheet 1A). Have a good reader read the parable aloud.

The parable is about a workhorse that finds out it's easier to be lazy than to pull his share of the load. Finally the farmer can put up with his sloppy work no longer and sends him out to pasture. For a while Sylvester has a wonderful time, but finally he gets bored with eating and running. His life no longer has a purpose. "If only I had another chance to show the farmer I've changed," he thinks, "I would make him so proud of me."

After kids have read the story, discuss the following questions:

Should the workhorse get another chance?

What if he messes up again?

The farmer's next move for Sylvester might be to the glue factory. How could Sylvester avoid that possibility?

Suppose God were the farmer, and Christians were the workhorses. How would you explain the meaning of the story?

Do you think God would give the failed Christian another chance?

2 HIGHLY TALENTED SERVANTS

Goal: That your students will discuss the Parable of the Talents and refute false statements about it.

Pass out copies of "The Talent Tale" (Action Sheet 1B). Read aloud the background given here:

The Talent Tale

Today when we say a person has talents, we mean he has abilities. But in Jesus' day, a person with lots of talents was rich. A talent was a large amount of money—equal to the total wages of a Jewish working man for almost 20 years. A talent was a fortune!

Even though the talents in the story we're going to look at today were money, Jesus wanted His listeners to apply the parable to much more than money. He wanted them to understand that talents were also abilities given to them by God. In fact, our English word *talent*, meaning ability, comes from this parable.

Jesus told the Parable of the Talents to His followers on the Mount of Olives just a few days before His crucifixion. He knew He would soon leave His disciples and He wanted them to be like the five-talent man and the two-talent man. He wanted them to make good use of their abilities to serve Him and draw more people into the Kingdom of God.

1. Now read the parable in Matthew 25:14-30. When you're finished, correct the three false statements below.

Have your kids work individually to correct the false statements. Then go over their answers together, using the additional discussion questions that follow. Suggested answers are given with the questions.

A. The five-talent man got praised because he had so many talents to begin with.

(The five-talent man was praised because he used what he had. That he made more talents than the others isn't the important point. What is important is that he took what he'd been given and used it as well as he could.)

B. The poor one-talent man didn't have a chance. He was set up to be a loser.

(To be a winner, the one-talent man would have to try and use what he had. After all, he did have one talent. It wasn't as though he hadn't been given anything at all. In fact, you might say his job was the easiest. In order to increase his talent by 100 percent as the other two servants did, all he had to do was make one more talent!)

Why did the master of the servants in this parable give various amounts?

(All the servants were given different amounts because Jesus wanted to illustrate that people differed in abilities. People have individual differences, and it is useless to compare one person with another.)

What kept the one-talent man from developing his talent?

(Fear. This servant was afraid of taking risks. He figured the safest thing to do was bury his talent. Maybe he made the mistake of comparing himself with the other servants, too. He figured he could never make as many talents as they could, so why try?)

How do you think the master would have responded to the one-talent servant if that servant had tried to increase his talent but had failed?

(He would have been far more pleased if the servant had even tried. And, chances are, if the servant had tried, he would have thought of some way to increase his talent. It might have even occurred to him to put it in a bank, and get interest on it, as the master suggested when he returned. Notice that the master *didn't* compare the one-talent servant with the other two servants!)

C. This parable teaches that the rich get richer and the talented automatically get more talented.

(This parable teaches that it's not how much you have, it's what you do with it that counts. The master never congratulates the servants for being "successful." He praises them, instead, for their faithfulness.)

2. If you just read verse 29, you could really get mixed up about what the Bible was teaching. But you have to read the Bible in chunks. One verse builds on the next; the whole thing fits together. Based on the whole parable, what does verse 29 mean?

(If we don't use our abilities, we may lose them. We never stand still. If we are not trying and hopefully moving forward, we must be moving backward. If we aren't trying to use the talents that we received from God, we must be losing any abilities we had.)

Kids may raise questions about verse 30. Does the use or nonuse of abilities affect one's eternal standing? It's important to remember that this is a parable, designed to make one main point: God expects us to use our opportunities and abilities in working for Him. Other details in the story can't be stretched. It would be fair to say, though, that the "worthless servant" is probably in the same category as the "subjects of the kingdom" in Matthew 8:12. They are people to whom favor was offered, but by their negligence they forfeited their right to it.

3. One more false statement to refute:

Not all Christians have talents.

(In the parable, each servant got something. The same is true for Christians. Everyone has something.)

You may be a one-talent person or you may be a five-talent person, but you are certainly not a zero-talent person. There just aren't any of those!

3 TALENT SEARCH

Goal: That your students will identify talents people have and will commit themselves to developing or further developing a talent in the next month.

If you feel you don't have any talents, part of the trouble may be that you wouldn't recognize a talent if you saw one. And you wouldn't know how to use it if you did spot it.

Divide your group into two teams. Each team is to think of Bible characters, what their talents or gifts were, and how they used those talents for God. Give kids five minutes to think of as many characters as they can.

Two points should be awarded for each character kids come up with. If teams duplicate each other's characters, they each get only one point, so kids should try to think of unusual characters.

Have teams take turns naming their characters. Keep score on a chalkboard, writing down each team's character, that character's ability, and how he or she used it. Continue until both teams have listed all the characters they thought of. You might want to award a small prize to the winners. Leave your list on the board.

Here's one example to get your kids started:

Character: Moses. Ability: talking with God; faith. How he used it: to save the Israelites from destruction many times.

Once you have your list on the board, ask kids the following questions:

These people used their talents. What reasons do we have for not using our talents?

(We are afraid of taking risks, just like the one-talent servant. We don't want to look dumb, and we don't want to fail.)

How can we overcome our fear of risk taking? Our Key Verse for today should help us with that.

Have your kids read I Peter 4:10:

"Each one should use whatever gift he has received to serve others, faithfully administering God's grace in its various forms."

This verse sums up the main reasons not to fear the risk of using a talent: because each of us has received some kind of gift; because

other people need to have us use our gifts; and because God has entrusted us with this gift and we don't want to disappoint Him.

Look at the list of abilities on the board. Are there any abilities there that remind you of a class member's talents?

Have each of your students tape a blank sheet of paper to the back of the person on his or her right. Have students move around the room and write on each person's paper what they think that person's abilities are. Caution kids to be serious, and to be sure they write something on each person's paper.

When kids have finished, have each one think about the abilities listed on his or her paper and how to develop those abilities. Give kids a few moments to think.

Encourage teens to commit themselves to work on one particular talent for the next month. Suggest that they write down *how* they are going to work on developing that talent. Let volunteers tell what talent they've chosen to work on and how they plan to do it.

After a few minutes, pass out envelopes and have each student write his or her name on the outside of the envelope. Then have kids seal their talent sheets into their envelopes. Collect the envelopes and let kids know that you'll distribute them in a month so that they can evaluate how they did on developing the talent they chose to work on.

Close your session by having kids pray sentence prayers, thanking God for the specific talents and abilities He has given members of the class.

HERE AM I, SEND ME?

Session Aim

That your kids will understand and respond to God's call to Christian service.

Key Verse

"Then I heard the voice of the Lord saying, 'Whom shall I send? And who will go for us?' And I said, 'Here am I. Send me!' " (Isaiah 6:8)

Things You'll Need

- *Bibles*
- *Pencils*
- *Paper*
- *"Trial Tasks" (Action Sheet 2A)*
- *"Called to Serve" (Action Sheet 2B)*
- *Chalkboard and chalk*

Most modern teenagers are familiar with calls. They get them on the telephone all the time!

That's not the only type of call there is, however. God calls people to glorify Him by doing His will. And He doesn't just call ministers, missionaries, and mental patients! He calls each of us to the task He has for us.

Use this session to help your kids see that God calls different people in different ways to different tasks. If we're following Him, He will call us. Kids and teachers alike need to seek what God will call them to do. When we're willing to serve Him, He'll have a place for us.

1
A CALL TO ACTION

Goal: That your students will discuss how they feel about having to complete some tasks.

Before your session, cut Action Sheet 2A, "Trial Tasks," into four separate task slips.

Announce to your kids that you would like some of them to serve God by completing some difficult tasks. Call four students to the front and give them the Trial Tasks slips. Tell them that they are not to speak to the other kids and that they must return within two minutes even if their tasks are not completed. Assign the four tasks, even if they cannot be completed within your setting.

While the four kids are off doing their tasks, explain to the rest of the class what the other kids are doing.

When the kids doing the tasks return, discuss the following questions.

How did you feel when you were called up here?

How difficult was your task?

Was it easier than what you expected when you came up here?

Why do people have doubts when they are called to do something? What's a healthy way to handle these doubts?

(Although God expects us to use our judgment in finding ways to serve Him, He often calls us to tasks that may seem beyond our abilities. He promises to supply what we need to do the job if we trust Him.)

What are some of your feelings when you think that God is calling you to work for Him?

God called the Old Testament prophets, who were normal human beings just like us. He had them do extremely difficult, even dangerous tasks. By trusting God to supply the know-how and courage, they agreed to do things they would never have tried to do on their own.

2 CALLING ALL PROPHETS!

Goal: That your students will investigate the responses of three prophets to God's call.

Our Bible study today focuses on three Old Testament prophets. They never had much chance to stop and consider how they would feel about being asked to do a difficult job. God called them when He was ready, and that was that! Sure, some of them were fearful and unsure of themselves, but they had enough faith in God to carry them through the most difficult assignments.

Begin today's study by passing out copies of "Called to Serve" (Action Sheet 2B). Read together the first paragraph on the sheet:

Called to Serve

God used different ways of communication with His prophets, but all of them got the message and responded.

Now divide your class into three groups, even if you only have groups of one. Give each group one assignment, and distribute paper and pencils.

Members of each group are to read the assigned Scripture, then answer the questions. To save time, a group might decide to divide the questions among the members, so that each member concentrates on one question.

Allow plenty of time for work on this study; then call the class together. Each group should be ready to report its findings to the rest of the class.

The assignments and suggested answers are included here for you. Be sure to work through the three assignments yourself before class so that you will be able to interact with the groups as they work.

Assignment One: The Call of Isaiah

Read Isaiah 6:1-11 and answer the following questions.

1. Suppose you had never before heard of God. What would you know about Him after reading this passage?

(This passage reveals much about God. It shows His all-encompassing glory and holiness. He takes the initiative in communicating with humans and revealing Himself. It shows His willingness to forgive—blot out sins and heal the repentant person. God works through people as His messengers. Though

God is patient in His dealings with people, He also punishes wrongdoing. Yet His punishment is constructive, followed by rebirth of faith and fellowship with Him.)

2. In what ways does Isaiah respond to God during this confrontation?

(In response to God's glory and holiness, Isaiah is filled with shame for his own sinfulness and that of his people. When God calls Isaiah to be His messenger, Isaiah responds in obedience and willingness. Confronted by the stubbornness of his people, Isaiah feels concern about their relationship with God.)

3. What instructions and preparation is Isaiah given for the work he will do?

(Part of Isaiah's preparation includes the sense of his own sinfulness and dependence upon God for forgiveness and strength. Because Isaiah has seen God's glory in a vivid way, He can preach about it more effectively to others. God also tells him what to say and prepares him for opposition.)

Assignment Two: The Call of Amos

Read Amos 7:10-17 and answer the following questions.

1. Suppose you had never before heard of God. What would you know about Him after reading this passage?

(We see here that God works through common people to communicate His Word. God's just wrath in punishing sin also comes through. He will not tolerate sin and idolatry indefinitely.)

2. Put yourself in Amos's place at the time of his call. What doubts and fears do you have about the work God has given you? What makes you agree to serve?

(Amos was a simple shepherd and farmer, probably with little prestige, power, or education. He doubted that he would know what to say to the leaders of Israel or that they would listen to him. Unlike Isaiah and Jeremiah, Amos had no formal religious training as a priest or prophet. Also, he was asked to preach in Israel even though he was from Judah. There was rivalry and hatred between those nations, and Israel would not welcome him.)

3. What evidence does this passage provide of Amos's faith and courage?

(Amos had the faith and courage to speak up to Amaziah, a priest who had access to the king himself. He did not draw back from boldly declaring God's Word.)

Assignment Three: The Call of Jeremiah

Read Jeremiah 1:4-19 and answer the following questions.

1. Suppose you had never before heard of God. What would you know about Him after reading this passage?

(God reveals Himself in history to His messengers and through them to His people. Even before their births, God designates His messengers and prepares them for the job. God strengthens and sustains those He calls and gives them the words to preach. He is in control of all nations and history. He punishes the unfaithful, often using other nations for His purpose.)

2. What assurance does this chapter provide for those called by God?

(God works through His chosen ones, in spite of their immaturity, faults, and weaknesses. God vindicates the messages of His prophets by making them come true. God gives His prophets the words to say and the courage to deliver them. God promises to protect His prophets from opposition.)

3. Put yourself in Jeremiah's place. How might you feel about delivering this message?

(He feels very unqualified for such an important mission because of his youth. He probably fears that people will laugh at him and refuse to listen, perhaps even try to kill him. Moreover, the prospect of doom for his country would be very painful.)

Have a student read the following wrap-up of today's study on the "Called to Serve" Action Sheet:

Our specific calls come when we commit ourselves to Christ. Jesus said, "If anyone would come after me, he must deny himself and take up his cross daily and follow me" (Luke 9:23). What this means is that when we commit ourselves to Him, He calls us to serve Him in whatever way we can.

In some cases God gives a person a special call as He did in the days of the prophets. These people know at a specific time and place what God is calling them to do, and they carry an extra responsibility with them.

No matter what we are called to do, either now or in the future, our lives should show the characteristics of a person who has accepted Christ's call to serve.

3 HERE AM I?

Goal: That your students will consider what God might be calling them to do.

Our Key Verse for this session suggests the kind of attitude God wants us to have toward serving Him.

Have your kids read the verse to themselves:

"Then I heard the voice of the Lord saying, 'Whom shall I send? And who will go for us?' And I said, 'Here am I. Send me!' " (Isaiah 6:8)

Are you ready to make the kind of commitment Isaiah made?

(Kids need not answer aloud unless they want to.)

If we're willing, we'll find many opportunities to work for God. Let's list some of them.

Have your kids suggest jobs God might call teenagers to do, and list their suggestions on a chalkboard. Give kids several minutes to brainstorm; then have kids stop and look over what you've written. Suggest that students pray for willingness to serve and for guidance in deciding how to serve. Have one student come up and mark the list for the whole class. Read the following instructions and help your class decide their responses to the instructions:

1. Place a check by all jobs you feel your class members could do with God's help.

2. Underline all jobs checked that you would be willing to do as a class.

Now have your student scribe rejoin the class and pass out paper. Then have each student follow these last instructions individually:

3. Write down one job that you *will* do.

4. List at least three steps you will take to accomplish your task.

Wrap up your class by letting kids know that you would be glad to help them get started on their commitments if they come to you for help.

Conclude with prayer that God will strengthen and guide each of you to serve according to His will.

STANDING UP

Session Aim

That your students will develop the desire to recognize and oppose social and spiritual problems.

Key Verse

"Let those who love the Lord hate evil, for he guards the lives of his faithful ones and delivers them from the hand of the wicked" (Psalm 97:10).

Things You'll Need

- *Bibles*
- *Pencils*
- *"The Contest" (Action Sheet 3A)*
- *"Decisions, Decisions!" (Action Sheet 3B)*
- *Chalkboard and chalk*

One doesn't have to look far to see evils in today's society. But imagine how those evils could multiply over the next decade if nothing is done about them. Imagine what the world might be like when your teens reach your age. Without a godly influence, our society will continue its downward slide.

God hates evil. He loves people even though they may be evil, but He hates evil. He hates it so much that He once used a flood to wipe the planet clean of nearly every sinful human being. He promised not to do that again, but that doesn't mean He doesn't care about the bad things He sees. Use this session to help your kids see the evil God sees, and to help them begin to do what they can to fight that evil. They won't turn the world to Christ overnight, but they can have an impact.

1 WHAT WOULD YOU DO?

Goal: That your students will talk openly on how they feel about opposing evil. Raise the following questions, and talk about them as a group. Try to involve all your students in the discussion.

Would you tell your parents about a friend who was selling drugs? Would you tell your school authorities?

Would you take the initiative in trying to lead the toughest kid in school to Christ? If not, why not?

If, while reading an assigned book, you came across material that you felt you shouldn't be reading as a Christian, would you read it? What would you do?

Do your friends at school know anything about what God is like from knowing you? Explain.

Talk openly about any of these questions that interest your kids.

Your kids will probably agree that a Christian should always stand for what is right and oppose that which is bad. But sometimes doing what's right is tough! And sometimes all the options seem bad. In cases like these, we've got to seek—with God's help—the best option.

Point out that our efforts to oppose evil will not always work. But a Christian is not asked to do what will "work." He is asked to do what is right. So sometimes we will have to work against things that are wrong, even if we don't see any way that our efforts will pay off.

2 JUST 450 AGAINST 2

Goal: That your students will analyze how they might have acted if they had been in Elijah's sandals.

Today's story is the culmination of one event in Elijah's action-packed life.

Distribute "The Contest" (Action Sheet 3A). Have one student read the opening paragraphs aloud. Then have kids read through the Scripture passages indicated. After kids have read the Scriptures, discuss the questions. The Bible study, additional questions, and suggested answers are included for you.

The Contest

Part I
Just as Elijah had prophesied, Israel was suffering through years of drought and famine. King Ahab and Queen Jezebel, in retaliation, had ordered the death of Elijah, but Elijah had escaped. They did not recognize that it was their own wickedness that had brought about the dry skies and barren fields.

One day, at the end of three years, Elijah sent a message for Ahab to meet him.

"You troublemaker!" Ahab said as Elijah greeted him.

"Don't blame me, Ahab, you're the one who worships Baal and ignores God's commandments."

Before the king could get a word in, Elijah went on. "If you want to settle this," he said, "have all the people meet me at Mount Carmel. Be sure that the 450 prophets of Baal are there."

Ahab agreed.

To find out what happened, read I Kings 18:20-40.

Part II
After the contest was over, Elijah killed all the prophets of Baal to make it harder for the people to revert to idol worship. God had demonstrated that He was in control.

Because Elijah had the courage to fight against evil, the Israelites—except for the wicked king and queen—were once more ready to repent and follow God.

Now have kids work individually or in groups to complete the questions in Part III; then have them report on what they discovered.

1. Why do you think all the water was poured on the sacrifice and in the trench?

(The people had to be convinced that this demonstration of power was not merely a magic trick. Even the fire had to be an unusual fire to consume water.)

2. What do you think the fire sent from Heaven proved?

(God does not need to "prove" anything, but the fire did demonstrate that He listens when His people call on Him. He is the God who is concerned about people. Actually He is the only God, but the people didn't really understand that. God also demonstrated that He is powerful enough to defeat any who oppose Him.)

3. Why do you think Elijah had the prophets of Baal killed? What principle for dealing with evil can we see in this?

Encourage discussion. Kids will probably point out that God doesn't want us to go around killing evil people. Rather, He wants us to fight injustice and evil without compromising. Elijah would not compromise; God expects the same from us.

Today's Key Verse talks about why God's people, like Elijah, cannot tolerate evil in any way and must oppose it when they see it:

"Let those who love the Lord hate evil, for he guards the lives of his faithful ones and delivers them from the hand of the wicked" (Psalm 97:10).

How is the Key Verse especially true of Elijah's life?

(God protected Elijah more than once, and in unusual or spectacular ways.)

How does this verse relate to Christ's command to love our neighbor? Do the two contradict each other? Explain.

(Like Elijah, the Lord hated evil. That's why He drove the money changers out of the Temple. Yet in His life, Christ demonstrated that we should also love. Each time He confronted evil on a personal level, He showed that He loved the sinner but hated the sin. He did this, for example, with the woman taken in adultery. He forgave the woman, but also told her not to sin anymore. In following Christ's example, we can consistently follow our Key Verse and the command to love.)

Elijah stood firm before wicked rulers who were leading the people of God away from God. He knew that such a stand could very well mean his death. In spite of the personal danger, he was willing to recognize and oppose evil when he saw it, and let God speak to the people through him.

3 THE NEED TO STAND

Goal: That your students will choose a way they can best stand against evil.

If we really take Elijah's example and our Key Verse seriously, we will want to go out and oppose social and spiritual problems around us. But it isn't easy.

Pass out copies of "Decisions, Decisions!" (Action Sheet 3B). Have your kids read about the fictional characters there to help them understand how hard it is sometimes to do what is right. Read each one and discuss it before moving on to the next one. Have kids comment on whether the actions of the individual involved were right or wrong. Ask them to tell what they would have done differently. The stories are reprinted here:

Decisions, Decisions!

Sometimes seeing what is right is easy, but doing it is hard. Other times it's hard to even see what is the right thing to do. Take a look at these fictitious characters and discuss what they did right and wrong.

Frederick Holmes ran a small store in rural Kentucky during the 1850s. When business was light he often read his Bible. After much prayer, he became sure that slavery was not right in the eyes of God. Yet many of his customers were slave owners. He began to talk to them about their sin. They scoffed. One night he heard a knock on his door. It was a black man, a runaway slave. Frederick Holmes knew it was not legal to hide runaway slaves, but he took the slave in. Soon others arrived, and Holmes did his best to get them to freedom, breaking the law time after time.

Mary Stephenson is a one-woman crusade against pornography. She has picketed bookstores and tried to talk to high school teachers who she thought were assigning reading from "dirty" books. She attends every city council meeting and started asking if she could address them on "the filth that is rampant in our city." One day they agreed to hear her out. She talked for 45 minutes and held up several examples of magazines that she felt should not be allowed to be displayed and sold in the city. When the mayor told her that the kind of ordinance she wanted was unconstitutional, she shouted that the Constitution should be changed if that was true.

Juan Venido is a low-level clerk in a major federal agency. About a year after he got his job, his boss asked him to "take care" of some money for him. At first Juan did what he was told, but when more and more money kept coming in, he got suspicious. It looked like something illegal was going on. One day he overheard a conversation that confirmed his suspicions. The next time his boss asked him to "take care" of some money, he refused. Later he learned that another clerk was doing it. Juan felt he should tell someone, but was afraid he'd lose his job. So instead of going to the police, he merely gave a "tip" to a newspaper reporter he knew. That night he prayed that someone would find out what was happening and put a stop to it.

Remind kids that it's often hard to know just how to respond to an evil situation.

We're likely to goof up the whole thing if we try to do it on our own. We've got to depend on God; He led Elijah, and He'll lead us, too.

Now divide your kids into groups of three or four. Have each group make a list of evils or problems they think Christians should try to correct in today's world. These may be spiritual, personal, social, or political. Combine your kids' lists on a chalkboard.

Discuss the following questions:

How did you decide what was an evil or a problem?

What standards did you apply in making your decisions?

If you were going to stand up against one of these evils, which one would you pick? Why?

What specific thing could you do to correct that wrong?

After discussing what *could* be done, encourage kids to each pick one thing to work on. If any kids are willing, let them tell what they've chosen. Then encourage kids to follow through on the actions they've chosen. Offer to help if you can.

Close your session with prayer, asking God to provide the courage your kids will need to take action against the evil in our world.

LITTLE THINGS MEAN A LOT

Session Aim

That your students will treat others as they would treat Christ Himself.

Key Verse

"The King will reply, 'I tell you the truth, whatever you did for one of the least of these brothers of mine, you did for me' " (Matthew 25:40).

Things You'll Need

● Bibles
● Pencils
● "Kindness Counts" (Action Sheet 4A)
● "A Very Important Animal Story" (Action Sheet 4B)
● Chalkboard and chalk

Our world isn't just selfish; it's turned selfishness into an art form! In our society, concern for others seems to have gone the way of the old-fashioned slide rule. "What will I get out of it?" is the question of the day.

Seldom do people go out of the way to do anything for anyone, with the possible exception of helping out a family member or a close friend. Very few would even consider doing something for a lowly stranger.

But is that the way Jesus wants Christians to be? Of course not. The passage we'll study in this session will make that clear. He wants us to see Him in every needy person and to treat that person accordingly. Use this session to help your kids learn to think a bit more about the needs of others—and a bit less about their own wants.

1 KINDNESS ROLES

Goal: That your students will participate in mini-dramas to show our careless treatment of other people.

Divide your kids into three groups, and give each group one of the situations from "Kindness Counts" (Action Sheet 4A). Each situation involves a Christian teenager who encounters an opportunity to do something kind for someone else.

Have each group work together to put on a brief skit portraying the situation on its sheet. Give kids a few minutes to plan; then have the skits presented one by one. At the end of each one, ask: "How would you react differently if the person you encountered were Jesus?" Discuss each skit briefly, and ask kids if they have ever rationalized their way out of helping in a similar situation.

The situations are printed for you here:

Kindness Counts

Susan
Susan is walking around in a crowded mall. Suddenly she spots Amanda, a girl in her class at school. Amanda hasn't seen Susan. Amanda is the leech type, but she looks lonely. Susan debates whether to go over and risk having Amanda follow her around the mall. She's just about decided to go over there when Amanda starts to turn in Susan's direction. Susan slips quickly around the corner, out of sight, and says to herself, "Aw, it doesn't matter anyway."

Jeff
Jeff is home alone reading a book. It's nearly lunchtime, and he's about to go downstairs to fix a sandwich when the doorbell rings. Looking out

the window of his second-story bedroom, he sees Mrs. Adleman standing on the front porch. He remembers hearing his mom say that Mrs.
Adleman was going to stop over
sometime collecting for the mission
hospital project. Mrs. Adleman
doesn't see Jeff at the window above.

Jeff debates: If he answers the door,
he'll have to give out of his own pocket. Mrs. Adleman will probably come
back when his folks are home, anyway. But he could save her the trip
by giving now. He just got his allowance and hasn't given any of it to
God yet. Jeff is still debating when
Mrs. Adleman turns to walk away.
Jeff shrugs and says to himself,
"Well, it doesn't matter anyway," and
heads downstairs to the kitchen.

Lynn
Lynn is hanging around the hall near
the phone booth after school with
some of her friends. A woman rushes
in and enters the phone booth. She
searches her purse, then opens the
door and says, "Do any of you kids
have change for a dollar?"

Lynn knows that she does, but for
some reason she just stands there.
She had saved that change in case
she wanted a candy bar on her way
home from school. Mary, a friend,
searches through her purse, but can
only find 75 cents. Lynn is just about
to reach for her purse when the woman says to Mary, "Well, here's the dollar, I'll take your 75 cents." Lynn
sighs and says, "Oh, well. She got
what she needed for the phone. It
doesn't matter."

After your discussions of the mini-
dramas, ask:

**What did these kids' behavior show
about how important they thought
the other people were?**

**Jesus told a parable that speaks
against having an uncaring attitude.
Let's take a look at it now.**

2 THE SHEEP AND THE GOATS

*Goal: That your students will evalu-
ate whether they are acting as
Christ would act.*

Have kids read through Matthew
25:31-46. You might want to have
them read it dramatically. Assign one
person to be the narrator and one to
be the King. Divide the rest of the
students into two groups: the goats
(those on the King's left) and the
sheep (those on the King's right).

**In verse 31, who is the "Son of
Man"? Explain this term.**

(This is a title for Jesus. He was not
only the Son of God, but He was also
the Son of Man. He lived on earth as
a human being.)

Pass out copies of "A Very Important
Animal Story" (Action Sheet 4B). Divide your kids into two groups, the
"sheep" and the "goats." The sheep
will answer the first question on the
sheet, and the goats will answer the
second. Instruct your kids to make

their answers as complete as possible. They are to look for what the passage means as well as looking for more easy-to-find facts.

Give kids a full five minutes to work on their observations. If some finish before the time is up, encourage them to go back and look for more.

A Very Important Animal Story

1. Read today's text and write down all the things you have learned about the people called sheep in this parable.

Kids will probably come up with many of the following observations.

● Sheep are people of the world—from all nations.

● Jesus knows who are sheep. He puts the sheep on the right. This seems to mean that this is a good place to be rather than the left. The word "but" seems to mean that the one is good and the other is bad.

● Jesus' Father loves the sheep, too.

● Jesus has been preparing a place for the sheep since the beginning of the world.

● Jesus mentions all the nice things the sheep have done for Him.

● The sheep did all these nice things without expecting to get credit for them. They didn't even remember the things.

● Jesus counts all the nice things His sheep do for other people as nice things they have done for Him.

2. Read Matthew 25:31-33, 41-46 and write down things you have learned about the people called goats in this parable.

● The goats are people of the world—from all nations.

● Jesus picks out the goats. They seem to be in trouble from the start because they are placed at His left.

● The goats will not be near Jesus. They are eternally separated from Him.

● Jesus is mentioned as having a throne of glory, but the goats belong in everlasting fire with the Devil and his angels.

● These people did not do any good things for Jesus. They did not belong to Him and He knew it.

● Both punishment and blessing is everlasting.

Have kids share their observations. Be sure kids see the point about Jesus' identification with the people the sheep helped.

Now go over the rest of the questions with your class.

Those sheep were really busy doing things for others. Jesus mentions six good deeds the sheep did. These good deeds stand for any service done in Christ's name, not just the six things mentioned.

3. These good deeds have some things in common. Name at least two of them.

(They are acts of kindness; they meet basic human needs; they are deeds anyone can do; they are done for individuals; they are done for people low in social standing.)

4. What might be two other examples of the kind of good deeds the sheep do?

Let kids suggest any kind of individual human needs they might see every day and would be able to meet.

Jesus is not saying that we can earn eternal life and become part of His family by doing good deeds. He is saying that when we serve others and lovingly give to them as part of our Christian service to Him, we are proving that we love Him.

What word in verse 34 shows that we don't earn eternal life?

(The word "inherit." Inheritance is due to being a member of a family, and doesn't depend on actions.)

People who aren't Christians do nice things, too, but these things aren't done for Jesus. Non-Christians don't belong to Him; they are still goats—often nice goats, but totally separated from God no matter how good they seem. Only as we admit our sin can we receive Christ's complete forgiveness.

6. Why were the goats surprised at their sentence?

(Like the Pharisees, they probably thought their lives were fine. They were doing some good deeds, weren't they? But they refused to realize that they were using their own standard to evaluate their goodness, rather than God's.)

If you are a sheep (Christian), God can actually use the service you do in the name of Christ as a way to turn goats (non-Christians) into sheep—to help non-Christians find Christ as Savior.

In today's parable we saw that Jesus considers Himself to be a physical, human brother of everyone in the world. So are we. In a human sense, we are brothers and sisters to every other human being. This huge family of people is made up of sheep and goats. Jesus cares about the goats just as He does the sheep. And He wants us to care about others the same way He does.

3 BEGINNING TO CARE

Goal: That your students will brainstorm a list of personal service project ideas and choose one to carry out.

Since Jesus wants us to treat others as we would treat Him, our goal should be to serve others. What project ideas can you think of for yourself, a small group of students, or our whole class?

Allow time for kids to discuss ideas, the feasibility of each suggestion, and actual plans to get involved in this project. List the possibilities on a chalkboard. Here are some questions to help your kids think of projects:

1. The first things Christ mentioned in today's Scripture were physical. Do you know someone who needs food?

2. Is there some specific thing that you know it would be right for you to do, but you've been putting off because it would take too much time, energy, money, etc?

3. Why not begin with your own family—what needs can you help meet there?

4. Do you know someone who has been hurt by rumors or unjust accusations who needs a supporting friend?

5. Do you treat your girlfriend or boyfriend as you would treat Christ?

6. Is there a friend of yours who doesn't know Christ? How can you tell or show that friend what Christ has done for you?

7. There are prisons in addition to those made of bricks and locks. Do you know someone held in a prison of shyness or ignorance whom you can reach?

After you have listed the possibilities, encourage your kids to each choose one project to work on this week.

Close your session with student prayer, if kids will pray. Suggest that each ask God to help him or her do a job that God would consider a success.

LOVE, JESUS STYLE

Session Aim

That your students will show Christ's love to others.

Key Verse

"This is how we know what love is: Jesus Christ laid down his life for us. And we ought to lay down our lives for our brothers" (I John 3:16).

Things You'll Need

• *Bibles*
• *Pencils*
• *Paper*
• *"Double Dilemmas" (Action Sheet 5A)*
• *"Paper Clips and Love" (Action Sheet 5B)*
• *Paper clips (three for each student)*

Jesus Christ seemed bent on avoiding the usual roads to success. Even people who hated Him could see that He was a spellbinding speaker, that He had talents far beyond the ordinary. Yet He didn't use these abilities to try to get in with the "in crowd"—the "important" people. Instead, He spent most of His time with the hurting, the needy. Some might say that Jesus wasted His talents working with the wrong people.

But Jesus was not operating on a success orientation. His whole ministry was based on love. And love dictated that He care for and meet the needs of those who needed Him. Christians today, including teenagers, need to follow Jesus' example of love. Use this session to challenge your kids to show Christ's love to the physically and emotionally needy kids around them.

1 LOVE IS . . .

Goal: That your students will role-play two scenes in which one person has to decide whether to serve another person in some way.

"Love" is a word that is used in so many different ways that it is often difficult to know exactly what is meant when we see or hear the term. Help your kids understand that true Christian love always involves serving others.

Be sure each student has a pencil and paper. Ask the following two questions, giving kids a chance to write down their answers. Tell kids to write down what they *would* do, not what they think they *should* do.

Suppose a close friend of yours calls at 11:30 p.m. and tells you that his parents have kicked him out of the house. What would you do?

Suppose a classmate you really don't like calls you at 11:30 p.m. and tells you that his parents have kicked him out of the house. What would you do?

After your kids have written their responses, use the role play, "Anne's Dilemma," from "Double Dilemmas" (Action Sheet 5A) to give your girls an opportunity to act out their responses. You be Anne, and have one of your class members play the part of Margo. Read the situation and then role-play a mock phone conversation. The first time through, explain that Margo is a close friend. Then choose another person to play Margo, and explain that this time she is a classmate Anne doesn't know very well and really doesn't like.

Use "Ted's Dilemma" from the same sheet for the guys in your group, switching the roles as with the girls. Repeat the role plays with other kids if you have time. The role play instructions are reprinted here:

Double Dilemmas

Anne's Dilemma
Margo's parents are separated, and her father lives 2,000 miles away. After a serious fight with her mother, Margo is ordered out of the house at 11:30 p.m. Not knowing where to go for help, she goes to a phone booth near her house and calls Anne, one of her classmates at school. To complicate things, Anne is planning to leave at 7:00 in the morning to go shopping with a couple of close friends. One girl's mother is planning to take them in their four-seat car.

Role-play Anne and Margo completing the phone conversation in the way you think you would respond in that situation.

Ted's Dilemma
Mike's parents are separated, and his father lives 2,000 miles away. After a serious fight with his mother, Mike is ordered out of the house at 11:30 p.m. Not knowing where to go for help, He goes to a phone booth near his house and calls Ted, one of his

classmates at school. To complicate things, Ted is planning to leave at 7:00 in the morning to go to a college football game with a couple of close friends. One guy's dad is planning to take them in their four-seat car.

Role-play Ted and Mike completing the phone conversation in the way you think you would respond in that situation.

After the role plays, discuss kids' responses.

Where did you see Christian love demonstrated in the role play? Give specific examples.

2 SCRIPTURE SCULPTURES

Goal: That your students will use Bible research and paper clip sculpture to illustrate that true Christian love always involves serving others.

What are some ways that Jesus showed His love for other people? Today's text from the Bible provides some answers to this question.

Pass out three paper clips to each student. Explain that today you will be working through the Scripture and the Bible study as a group. Pass out copies of "Paper Clips and Love" (Action Sheet 5B). Follow this guide for additional questions and suggested answers. Call on different kids to give answers, and have all the kids explain their three paper clip sculptures.

A note about paper clip sculpture: This kind of Bible study may be new to you. Most teachers are accustomed to words. They want kids to respond in writing or in speaking. But what about the kids who are not good at writing or speaking? Paper clip sculpture puts everyone on the same level. It allows kids to give their answers nonverbally. So give it a try—you may be surprised who does well.

Paper Clips and Love

1. Overpopulation, famine, disease, and crime are everywhere. What is a Christian supposed to do in the face of all these pressing needs?

2. Read Matthew 9:35-38. Take your first paper clip and twist it into a sculpture illustrating one quality Jesus showed toward others in this passage.

Some qualities that might be illustrated are pity, authority, willingness to go out to where the people were, ability to teach, ability to preach, ability to heal.

One sculpture kids might make is a pair of wings, illustrating movement: Christ was willing to move out to help people.

3. Consider what Christ did as He traveled through the cities and villages of His land. List persons or groups of persons who are doing some of these same things in our day.

(Christ taught. People doing this today would be Sunday School teachers, parents, leaders of Bible studies, and Christian teachers in schools and colleges. In one sense, every Christian should be a teacher by the example of his or her life.

(Christ preached. Pastors, youth speakers, and evangelists are doing this today.

(Christ healed. In our day, doctors, nurses, rescue workers, and people who help sick friends and relatives are involved in healing. It is also apparent that God sometimes heals people in miraculous ways.)

4. Read Matthew 10:1, 7, 8. In verses 7 and 8, the Lord directed the disciples to be active in five areas as they contacted people. List each area.

(Preaching, healing the sick, making lepers clean, raising the dead, driving out demons.)

5. Take a close look at these five areas and then summarize what must have been Jesus' idea of evangelism. (Hint: How does Jesus relate physical needs to spiritual needs?)

Help kids with this summary if they have trouble. One summary might be as follows: For Jesus, to evangelize means to be concerned about a person's total needs. Kids might also note that Jesus had others help Him in this work.

What might have happened if Jesus had separated the spiritual needs from the physical needs of the people and only dealt with the spiritual ones?

(People may not have listened to Him due to their anxiety about their physical needs. The people might have become bitter toward Him, feeling that

He really didn't care about them. They would have doubted that He was the Messiah because an Old Testament prophet prophesied that the Messiah would heal.)

6. Read I John 3:16-18. Take your second paper clip and illustrate one important principle Christians should find in this passage.

Kids may illustrate the principle that love is willingness to share our material possessions with those in need. Someone might bend a clip to represent an extra hat that could be given to someone who needs one. Someone else might make a heart.

Verse 16 is today's Key Verse:

"This is how we know what love is: Jesus Christ laid down his life for us. And we ought to lay down our lives for our brothers" (I John 3:16).

If we are going to lay down our lives for our brothers, it is important to know who our brothers are. Who are our brothers?

Let kids speculate.

From what you know of the life of Christ, whom did He treat as His brother?

(Christ had a special relationship with those who accepted Him and followed Him. However, He always seemed to reach out to everyone. Sometimes He was rejected but at least He tried. So it seems that even though we should be particularly sensitive to the needs of our Christian brothers and sisters, we should consider everyone to be our neighbor.)

7. Most people have not had the opportunity to lay down their lives for others. However, God has defined this sacrifice of laying down one's life in a practical way that every Christian has the opportunity to carry out. According to verse 17, what is a practical way one's life can be laid down for others?

(If I see someone in need, I should share with that person.)

8. True love is more than a warm feeling. What yardstick does God use when He evaluates our love?

(God does not evaluate our love by our words and our talk. He evaluates our love by how it shows up in our actions. That is the meaning of verse 18.)

9. Now take your last paper clip and illustrate one of the ways you could put love into action.

Someone might bend a paper clip to represent the dead branches he or she could pick up from an elderly neighbor's yard.

As kids tell about their bent clips, encourage them to be as specific as possible about things they could do.

Jesus showed His love by serving others. His disciples followed His example. We can follow His example, too.

3 ACTING ON LOVE

Goal: That your students will plan one way to show their concern for others this week.

Before your session, decide which of the following service ideas will work best for your group.

1. Group Project

Divide your class into groups of four or five. Instruct each group to develop a project the entire class could do together. The purpose of this project is to exercise Christian love by serving others in need. Make sure your kids keep it practical.

Have the groups present their projects to the class. Then class members can decide which one they would like to choose as a class project. Make any initial plans you can for getting the project started.

2. Individual Project

Instruct each student to think of one way he or she can show Christian love this week. After kids have chosen one thing, they should plan exactly how they are going to carry out this personal project. Encourage each one to write this out. After each student has planned how he or she will demonstrate Christian love this week, it would be good for the class to divide into pairs so each student can share his or her plan with one other person. Each pair should pray for one another during the week.

3. Prayer Project

Each student should develop a list of people he or she is concerned about. This list will not be shared with the rest of the class. These could be sick neighbors or friends, older people, unemployed acquaintances, and so on. Often prayer is the first step to becoming actively involved in serving others.

Close your session with silent prayer. Suggest kids pray daily this week, asking God what He might have them do. Encourage kids to be willing to follow through with any ideas God might bring to them for service.

A LESSON IN HUMILITY

Session Aim

That your students will discover how to be humble in everyday situations.

Key Verse

"Young men, in the same way be submissive to those who are older. All of you, clothe yourselves with humility toward one another, because, 'God opposes the proud but gives grace to the humble.' Humble yourselves, therefore, under God's mighty hand, that he may lift you up in due time" (I Peter 5:5, 6).

Things You'll Need

● *Bibles*
● *Pencils*
● *Paper*
● *Markers*
● *"Servant Savior" (Action Sheet 6A)*
● *"Humility Is . . ." (Action Sheet 6B)*
● *Optional: Basin of water, towel*

For most people, humility doesn't come naturally. We love to have people rave about things we've done or how wonderful we are. And it's very easy to become proud.

But Jesus, who of all people was most deserving of glory, humbled Himself. First He became human; then He washed His followers' feet; then He died a humiliating, sacrificial death on a cross. He could have demanded a royal arrival on earth, or that mankind wash His feet, or that His executioners never be forgiven. But He didn't.

This session concentrates on how Jesus washed His disciples' feet to give us an example of the humility He talked about. He showed us that no one, not even the Son of God, is too good to be a servant. Use this lesson to help your kids put their own worth into perspective and to begin serving others as Jesus wants them to.

1 THE COLOR OF PRIDE

Goal: That your students will create symbolic representations of pride.

Provide paper, along with marking pens in a variety of colors, for your kids. Ask each student to draw a symbol representing pride, using what he or she feels is the appropriate color. After kids have drawn their symbols, have them write explanations of the symbols on the same sheet of paper. Here is a sample explanation:

(I chose the color red because I think of pride as something that is showy or flamboyant, calling attention to itself. I used this symbol, looking somewhat like a thistle, because I think of proud people as being prickly—not the kind you want to get close to. Rather obnoxious, actually.)

Have kids display their symbols and read their explanations. As each student speaks, write on a chalkboard the characteristics of pride which are described. Here are some possibilities:

(Rudeness, selfishness, giving only to get something in return, giving only so others will think well of you, constantly comparing your good deeds with the good deeds of others, not doing things for fear of making a mistake.)

Point out the obvious—the characteristics of pride are not exactly ones which Christians should try hard to acquire! Remind kids that humility, the opposite of pride, is one goal of the Christian. Then paraphrase the following paragraph:

Humility is not putting yourself down. It is not weakness. Instead, humility is a willingness to use your abilities to serve others.

Unfortunately, it is much easier to demonstrate pride than it is to demonstrate humility. Humility is hard work.

2 A LESSON IN SERVICE

Goal: That your students will participate in an inductive Bible study of John 13:3-5.

Explain that the events in the Scripture you're studying today took place just before the Feast of the Passover. Jesus was soon to die on the cross. But He still had a few important lessons to teach His disciples while He was on earth. One of the big lessons was in humility.

Distribute copies of "Servant Savior" (Action Sheet 6A), and divide the class into pairs. Give each pair a sheet of paper and a pencil, and allow about 15 minutes for study of the passage. Make sure kids write down what they find, because they will report on their findings later. Encourage them to look for things that others might not see, and to make application of the things that they find.

Do this study for yourself right now, before you study the rest of the lesson. Then, to add to your own discoveries, the lesson includes some of the ideas your kids may find.

During class, move from pair to pair. If the conversations are too shallow, ask a question to take the pair deeper. If someone is being left out, ask him or her a question.

The study, suggested comments, and extra questions are included here for you.

Servant Savior

Read John 13:3-15, and then answer the following questions.

1. What things can you learn about Jesus from this passage?

(Jesus was aware that He had come from God—that He was God.

(Jesus' humility came from strength.

(He knew who He was and yet He was willing to serve others.

(It's interesting that Jesus' powerful position is established in verse 3 before His act of humility begins in verse 4. He listened and answered His disciple's question.

(Jesus does not always make everything clear to us immediately. Peter, for example, wouldn't totally understand that Jesus was talking about spiritual cleanness in verse 8 until after the Resurrection.

(Jesus knew the conditions of His disciples' hearts. He knew that all but one would follow Him.

(Jesus accepted His role as Lord and Master of men.

(Jesus told His disciples to follow His example.

(He was perfectly willing to be a servant. He did the foot washing without anyone telling Him to.

(Jesus explained the plan of salvation here, but indirectly. Unless a person is washed of sin by Jesus, that person would never be able to be His disciple.

(Jesus was able to use very human things—like washing feet—to teach great spiritual lessons.)

2. What things can you learn about the Christian life from this passage?

(Jesus doesn't expect us to always understand everything immediately. He didn't get mad at Peter for not knowing and understanding completely what He was doing. Perhaps since we now have the complete Bible and understand that the Resurrection really did happen, Christ expects us to have greater understanding than Peter did at this point in his life.

(When Jesus washes our lives, we are clean in His sight.

(Jesus expects His disciples to accept Him as Master and Lord.

(Jesus expects us to follow His example. This means that we are to serve others as He served others. This may take the form of washing someone's dirty feet or it may take the form of any other kind of service. After all, the final service of Christ was hinted at in verse 3. He would die for people's sins.)

3. What title would you give this passage to distinguish it from all other Scripture? Write your title above the passage.

(Some possibilities: How to Be a Christian Servant; A Message in Humility; Foot Washing and Other Ways to Serve People.)

4. In what way could you apply the messages in these verses to life today?

Pay close attention to what your students say here. It will tell you exactly what they have learned.

As kids relate to the total class what they consider to be their major points, ask additional questions to draw them out. Clarify any difficult points. Compliment people who really have hit on unusual and difficult truths from this passage. Add things which you found.

What if Jesus had been proud instead of humble? How do you think this would have affected His ministry?

(The common people, including the 12 disciples, would not have been attracted to Him. Influential people rejected Him even though He was humble. If He had been proud, though, this would have given them ammunition to call Him a hypocrite.)

In verse 15, Jesus tells His disciples to follow His example. Look at the verse. Peter, for one, must have taken Christ seriously. In one of Peter's letters to other Christians, he says some profound things about humility. Let's read our Key Verses for today:

"Young men, in the same way be submissive to those who are older. All of you, clothe yourselves with humility toward one another, because, 'God opposes the proud but gives grace to the humble.' Humble yourselves, therefore, under God's mighty hand, that he may lift you up in due time" (I Peter 5:5, 6).

Paul and James, like Peter, also wrote about humility. Let's look at the statements of these three writers more closely.

Assign one of the passages listed under question 5 to each of the study pairs. After your kids have completed their answers, discuss them.

5. Write two or three key statements about humility that you can draw from the Scripture passage below which is assigned to you. For example, a key statement from the passage where Jesus washed the disciples' feet might be, "Humility expresses itself in service to others." Each pair will report its findings to the group.

I Peter 5:1-6

James 4:6-10

Philippians 2:4-11

Here are some possible key statements that your kids might discover:

I Peter 5:1-6

(The humble person leads by example. Humility leads to serving one another. God gives more grace—undeserved favor—to the humble. In due time, God will exalt [reward] those who humble themselves before God.)

James 4:6-10

(God gives more grace—undeserved favor—to the humble. To be humble, you must submit to God and resist Satan. The proper way to approach God is with an attitude of humility.)

Philippians 2:4-11

(Humility is based on a proper understanding of who you are. Humility is based on a proper understanding of who God is. Humility is not ambitious. Humility is directly linked to obedience.)

Discuss your kids' answers, then move on to the next section.

3 HAVING HUMILITY

Goal: That your students will participate in hand washing, symbolically indicating their willingness to serve others humbly.

Pass out copies of "Humility Is . . ." (Action Sheet 6B), and have kids read over the cartoons there. Ask kids which ones they can relate to most closely. Discuss how hard it is to do some of the things suggested in the cartoons.

Now ask kids to close their eyes and personally think through the following questions. They do not need to vocalize their answers.

In today's lesson, Jesus wasn't just talking about washing feet. Obviously, washing feet was a symbol of all kinds of dirty, unattractive, difficult service that we, as Christians, might be called to do.

What kinds of jobs might you be too *proud* to do for Christ?

On the other hand, which jobs would be hard to do because they're considered lowly?

For instance, would you be willing to make friends with an unpopular person? Would you be willing to baby-sit for free for a family who needed it? Would you be willing to . . . ? Mentally complete this sentence with the most difficult thing God could ask you to do for others.

If you think your kids will seriously participate in the following activity, it can be very meaningful.

Set a basin of water and a towel on a table. Explain that as a symbolic expression that they are willing to serve others—even if it means humbling themselves and doing the dirty jobs—they will have an opportunity to participate in a hand-washing service.

Ask volunteers to come up to the table, one at a time, take the bowl to another student, dip that student's hands into the bowl, and dry them.

The student should then pray, asking the Lord to help him or her become humble enough to be a servant to others. When one student finishes, another should come and get the bowl and go through the same procedure. No student's hands should be washed twice if it means that others are left out. When it is clear that all students who wish to participate have done so, follow the same procedure yourself, and close in prayer.

If you don't think your kids can seriously do the above activity, spend some time discussing things they can do to show humility and an attitude of service. Challenge kids to take action on those things this week. Close by praying that kids will show their humility in their actions each day.

TO THE ENDS OF THE EARTH

Session Aim

That your students will share in their responsibility for worldwide evangelism.

Key Verse

"He said to them, 'Go into all the world and preach the good news to all creation'" (Mark 16:15).

Things You'll Need

● *Bibles*
● *Pencils*
● *Paper*
● *Missions display*
● *"Other People, Other Places" (Action Sheet 7A)*
● *"Reporter's Notebook" (Action Sheet 7B)*
● *Aerogram (optional)*
● *City or area map (optional)*

During the nearly 2,000 years since Jesus gave the command at the end of His earthly ministry, Christians have been trying to spread their faith to every part of our world. In the last century, a burst of missionary work has sent missionaries from North America to nearly every country possible. Now some Third World countries are sending out missionaries of their own.

Worldwide evangelism is one important form of service. Do your kids know much about it? What are their feelings toward workers who are carrying God's message of salvation to those who haven't heard it?

Your students may have been to a missions conference or heard a few missionary speakers, but most teens probably feel that world missions has little to do with them. Use this session to help acquaint your kids with a real missionary, and to challenge them to do their part in spreading the Gospel to the world.

1 MISSIONARY PROFILE

Goal: That your students will discuss a missionary's work using information from your own church.

Before your session, prepare a poster or bulletin board display about one or more missionaries supported by your church. Include things such as a map showing missionaries' locations, a prayer letter, and pictures of missionaries engaged in various activities. Let kids study this display; then distribute pencils and paper. Ask kids to jot down answers to the following questions.

Why do you think _____ chose this career?

(Refer to the missionary or missionaries by name, and continue to do so throughout the session.)

What special personality traits, skills, or abilities do you suppose he or she needs for this work?

What sort of activities do you imagine _____ performs in a typical day?

What do you think you might have in common with _____?

How do you think you would like it if you could spend a typical day with him or her?

If there is time, have your students share their answers aloud.

If there is any possibility of having a missionary visit your class, this would be an excellent day to do it.

This week's session is going to be about the very first "official" foreign missionaries—Barnabas and Paul. We may well find, as we get into our study, that Barnabas and Paul and _____ and you and I, have more in common than we realize!

2 ON THE ROAD WITH PAUL AND BARNABAS

Goal: That your students will chart the events surrounding the sending of the first missionaries, Paul and Barnabas.

The apostle Paul was a man used greatly by God in many different ways. Today we're going to take a look at his partnership with Barnabas in a brand-new venture.

We're going to look at Acts 13, which begins a section of the book specifically on the actions and travels of Paul. Let's look at today's Scripture.

Pass out copies of "Other People, Other Places" (Action Sheet 7A). Have your kids read Acts 13:2-5, 42-46. Then read through what could be Paul's view of the events in this passage. The text from the Action Sheet is printed for you here.

Other People, Other Places

There I was attending the Antioch Church when the Lord told some of the prophets and teachers who also attended there that Barnabas and I had been called for a special work. The Holy Spirit wanted us to preach in foreign lands!

Well, you can imagine what a thing like that did to my prayer life: sped it up, fast! Why, we didn't even know where to go, how to get there, or what to do once we got there! I mean, we were the first missionaries ever sent. The very first!

When we docked at Salamis, I heaved a sigh of relief. Salamis, being the most important town on the island, had a good-sized Jewish population, and was I glad to see that! Setting off for lands unknown can be mighty scary without a friendly face.

Barnabas and I headed for the synagogues (there were several in town) and preached the news about Jesus. After that we started working our way across the island. One hot, sweaty afternoon we finally made it all the way to Paphos, the capital. Things had gone well, and we were getting brave. So we decided to go see the governor of the island.

We got in to see him all right, but he had a man with him who claimed to be religious. The guy pulled off all sorts of mystical tricks.

I thought he was going to spoil everything, but God performed a miracle through me and struck him blind. You should have seen the governor (or proconsul, as he was called) sit up at that!

We sailed from there to Perga in Pamphilia. (You probably call it Turkey.) Barnabas and I started hiking through the hills to the town of Antioch (not the same Antioch we started out from). Besides, the coastal region around Perga was pretty thick with mosquitos, mostly the malaria-carrying kind.

We headed for the synagogue in this new town of Antioch and told them the story of Jesus and God's love. Well, the people said to come back next week and tell them more. So we did. Of course, we invited most of the rest of the town, too.

When the local Jews saw all those Gentiles, they were furious! Seems they wanted the Good News for themselves.

I told them that I'm a Jew, too. That's why I came to them first. But, I said, you can't expect to keep God for yourself! He's for everybody!

When I tried to speak, the Gentiles and many of the Jews rejoiced with me. However, some Jews walked out.

I could have cried. My own people! Don't they know our God is the God of the whole world?

Because of the significance of this important journey Paul and Barnabas made, your students should find out more about the passage we're studying. So guide your group through the following in-depth study of the passage.

Let's suppose we are all reporters assigned to do an article on the experiences of Paul and Barnabas told about in Scripture.

If you have more than five kids, divide into two or three groups for this activity. Ask each group of reporters to make up a name for the newspaper it is working for.

Examples might include *The Antioch Announcer, The Seleucian Sun-Times, The Salamis Signpost,* or even *The Rome Recorder.* But don't let the groups dwell too long on name selection. The research is the important part of this exercise.

As reporters, the first thing we have to do is be sure we have our facts straight. We need to know answers to the journalistic questions—Who? What? To or for Whom? How? When? Where? Why?

Distribute copies of "Reporter's Notebook," Action Sheet 7B.

The chart on this action sheet will help you get the facts. Fill it out. You can look back at the Scripture and "Other People, Other Places" as often as you want.

As your reporters work on their research, you may want to circulate among the kids to offer any help that might be needed. The chart, including answers, is reprinted on the next page.

If kids seem to have trouble answering any questions, encourage them to look up the verses in a variety of Bible versions. If there is a question that doesn't seem to be answered in a particular verse, tell your students to put a line there and to go on to another question or verse.

When the kids have finished their research, ask them to tell what they have found. You might want to have a blank chart copied on a chalkboard or a large sheet of paper. Fill in the chart with the answers as students give them.

If your class does not enjoy written activities or has trouble with Bible study, you could read each verse and ask volunteers to answer each of the journalistic questions. Then, as students answer, you could fill in the information on the chart.

After going over the chart, ask this question:

Why do you think Paul and Barnabas became missionaries?

Let kids respond.

Our Key Verse for today gives us a better understanding of the "why" behind their action. So let's read it:

"He said to them, 'Go into all the world and preach the good news to all creation' " (Mark 16:15).

3

A MIND FOR MISSIONS

Goal: That your students will discuss ways they can presently take an active role in missions.

Let's think about Paul and Barnabas for just a little longer. Quickly look over your charts and see if you can find some things these first official missionaries have in common with missionaries today.

What are some differences between Paul and Barnabas and the missionaries that go out from our churches today?

What do most of us have in common with Paul and Barnabas and our modern missionaries?

Sometimes we forget that we're called to be missionaries just as much as Paul and Barnabas and the

missionaries that go out from our church. **We all have a responsibility to do what we can in missions both nearby and far away.**

To help your kids start taking action on what you've studied, go over the following Plan A with them, helping them choose what they might be able to do in the missions ministry of your church. Or take them through the exercise described in Plan B.

Plan A
There are many projects you can do to encourage missionaries. Here are just a few possibilities you might consider:

● **Maybe you enjoy Christian magazines and magazines on sports, fashion, and teen news. Missionary kids do, too. Why not send a gift subscription of your favorite Christian magazine?**

● **Write a round-robin letter. Pass around an aerogram, and let everyone at church or in your Sunday School class write a few lines. This saves wear and tear on your pen and lets the missionary know a lot of people care. (Note: An aerogram is a special letter that folds up to make its own envelope. Get several from the post office. Postage is several cents cheaper than sending airmail stationery in an envelope!)**

● **Eat-a-thon. Ask missionaries to send you recipes from their countries. Plan a church dinner featuring the recipes. Have people give a donation at the dinner, and send the proceeds to the missionaries.**

Plan B
Put up a large map of the area. If there aren't printed maps available,

you can draw a rough map of your own. Pass out two small slips of paper to each student and give the following instructions:

Since all of us are called to be missionaries to spread the Good News of Jesus, the area where we live should be our first mission field. So I've brought this map of our mission field.

On one slip of paper, write one way you can spread Christ's message in our community. It could be something you might do at school, church, home, or anywhere else in the area.

If some kids think of several ways they could be missionaries in their own community, encourage them to fill out more than one slip.

As the slips are completed, have kids tape them to the map in the appropriate location. If it's something they can do at school, have kids tape it at the school's location on the map.

When the map is dotted with lots of slips, your kids should realize the number of ways they have to serve God right in their own community. Encourage them to choose one or more ideas and carry them out.

As you close your class, pray specifically for any missionaries or missionary projects you talked about during this session. Ask the Lord to guide all of your students in their efforts to be missionaries to their own community. And also pray that the Holy Spirit will lead each of your students into an area of service that is in God's will.

SESSION 8 SHARING CHRIST

Session Aim

That your students will take advantage of every opportunity to witness with enthusiasm and skill.

Key Verse

"Do you not say, 'Four months more and then the harvest'? I tell you, open your eyes and look at the fields! They are ripe for harvest" (John 4:35).

Things You'll Need

● Bibles
● Pencils
● Paper
● "What's It All About?" (Action Sheet 8A)
● "To Sow and Reap" (Action Sheet 8B)
● 3" x 5" cards

One of the toughest things for many Christians to do is to serve others by telling them about Jesus. Fear of rejection often gets in the way of our good intentions.

One way to get people to witness is to make them feel guilty. But guilt may not produce very effective witnessing. A better motivation is gratitude. God has done so much for us in providing salvation, we should naturally want to tell others about the gift we have received.

Not knowing how to witness is another obstacle. But a simple testimony and a very brief presentation of the Gospel can be extremely effective when given naturally and sincerely. Use this session to help your kids learn how to tell friends what Christ has done for them and what He can do for others.

1 BASKETBALL EVANGELISM

Goal: That your students will begin thinking about what it means to witness for Christ.

Today's session focuses on Christ's call to His followers to be effective witnesses for Him. Pass out copies of "What's It All About?" (Action Sheet 8A) Your kids will enjoy reading this true account of what one church in Tennessee did for the young people in its community.

After kids finish reading, discuss the following questions.

The minister who wrote this article admits that "16-year-old Jerry Williams" gave him the best "sermon" he'd ever heard. What do you think was the message of that sermon? Explain.

Name at least one principle about witnessing to others that you get from this article.

Conclude this section by paraphrasing the following paragraph:

Everybody needs to hear the story of Jesus Christ and the redemption He brings. That's why witnessing is an important way to serve people. Some churches witness with a basketball team. Others witness in other ways. The main thing is that we communicate this important message. Jesus talks about this in our Scripture lesson today.

Let's discover what He has to teach us.

2 A MESSAGE TO SHARE

Goal: That your students will identify the major points of the message of salvation.

Be sure each student has a Bible and a pencil. Pass out copies of "To Sow and Reap" (Action Sheet 8B), and have kids go through the study individually. Pass out cards for kids to use for question 6. When kids have answered the questions, go over their answers together. The study is printed for you here, along with possible answers and additional discussion questions.

To Sow and Reap

1. To give you some background for the passage we'll study today, read John 4:6-30 and write a title describing this story.

(Some possible titles: "Living Water"; "Could This Be the Messiah?"; "Jesus Witnesses to a Foreigner.")

Why do you think Jesus asked the woman for a drink?

(It was an opportunity to start a conversation in a natural way.)

You might want to mention to your kids that Samaritans and Jews usually refused to speak to one another due to a deep mutual hatred.

Not only was the woman at the well a Samaritan, she also had a bad reputation. Why do you think Jesus even wanted to talk with her?

(Jesus saw this as an opportunity to offer her the water of life. He knew that it was urgent that He take advantage of every opportunity to share His message.)

Why do you think the woman responded to Jesus?

(Instead of emphasizing her faults and sins, Jesus talked about something that the woman was interested in—water—and used that as a natural bridge to tell her who He was.)

What principles from this story can you apply to a situation where a Christian should share his or her faith in Christ with a non-Christian?

You might want to write students' suggestions on the board. Here are some thoughts on the subject.

(1. We must begin where people are. Jesus began with the well and water. We must talk about things people are interested in and concerned about. We must use illustrations that they can understand.

(2. We must make opportunities. Jesus went from waterpots to eternal life. In a natural way, we must learn to turn ordinary conversation into opportunities to share Christ.

(3. We must accept people's differences and not condemn them or look down on them for their sins and their mistakes.)

In this incident Jesus provided for all of us a living example of how we,

as His followers, should be witnesses for Him. When He shared the message of the Word of Life with the Samaritan woman, He illustrated how we can be lights to the world.

Jesus then gave His disciples some valuable advice concerning the importance and urgency of witnessing. Let's look at what you discovered about this advice in the next question on your sheets.

2. Now read John 4:31-41 and write a title explaining the key message found there.

(Some possible titles are: "When Food Didn't Matter"; "A Harvest Takes Two"; "The Fields Are Ripe for Harvest!")

3. In explaining His message to the disciples, Jesus used some terms to symbolically communicate to them what He wanted them to learn from this situation. What did Jesus mean by His use of the following words?

a. Food

(Jesus explained that He received nourishment that the disciples did not know about. His energy came from His obedience to His Father rather than simply from physical food. To Jesus, obedience to God meant sharing with others a message of eternal life.)

Why do you think Jesus refused physical food at this time?

(There were people coming from the village to visit Him. It was urgent that they be given the message of eternal life. Perhaps He was so involved in His true ministry that He didn't feel hungry. There would be time for food later.)

b. Fields

(Jesus talked to His disciples about the great number of people who had heard the Good News. He compared these people to a field or crop that is waiting to be harvested.)

c. Harvest

(Of those who had heard the message, only certain ones would actually accept it. The harvest is the people who accept and receive Christ.)

d. The reaper

(The one who reaps represents the Christian who actually has the opportunity of leading someone else to Christ.)

4. Explain what Jesus meant when He was talking about the reaper and the sower.

(Often when a person becomes a Christian he has had many contacts with the Good News of salvation from many different sources. The reaper is the person who actually leads the non-Christian to make a decision for Christ. The sowers [planters] are all the people who were able to share Christ with this person in some way.)

Why do you think Christ used this illustration of the planter and the reaper?

(It was an illustration that the disciples would understand. They knew about the teamwork and cooperation that it took to plant and harvest a field. They could easily apply this knowledge to the spiritual harvest.)

5. If Jesus had been talking to a group of city people, what symbolic illustration might He have used?

Let your kids speculate. If you have time, let kids develop their illustration ideas into more complete illustrations to parallel the one you've been studying.

6. The Samaritans believed in Jesus for two reasons. First there was the testimony of the woman. Second, and more important, was the message of Jesus. Obviously the same is true today. People become interested in Christ and perhaps even decide to believe in Him by watching the lives of Christians and by listening to their testimonies of what Christ has meant to them.

But included in the personal testimony is Christ's message of salvation.

On a small card, write a brief outline of Christ's message of salvation as you understand it. Use Bible references wherever possible. Some you might want to use are Romans 3:23; 6:23; 10:9; John 3:16; 10:10; I John 5:11.

Have your kids work in pairs to list the major points involved in Christ's message of salvation. After two or

three minutes, begin to compile these points on a chalkboard and work them into a good outline of salvation. Encourage kids to add Scripture references for each major point.

This list of major points in the plan of salvation is a tool you can use to lead others toward faith in Christ. Jesus considered this task so urgent that on at least one occasion, He didn't eat because He had an opportunity to witness instead. Let's practice using this tool right now so that we will be better prepared when we are presented with opportunities to witness.

3 PUTTING IT INTO PRACTICE

Goal: That your students will practice sharing the Good News of salvation.

Have your kids work in pairs again. Spread them out so that each pair will have as much privacy as possible. Instruct each pair to choose one of the situations from question 7 on Action Sheet 8B.

7. Practice sharing the message of salvation with a partner. Choose one of the situations below. Be sure to be sensitive, tell about Christ's message, and include your own personal testimony.

● A close friend of yours is in the hospital as a result of a motorcycle accident.

● A friend has come to church for the first time.

● A parent or neighbor has asked you some questions about the salvation message.

First, one student should assume the role of a Christian while the other plays the role of a non-Christian. After about three minutes, have them reverse roles. The non-Christian may want to raise questions or objections that might be raised in a real witnessing situation. But encourage kids not to get carried away with their objections.

If time permits, share the following witnessing techniques—good and bad—with your students.

Poor Witnessing Techniques
1. Attacking another person's beliefs instead of simply presenting Christ.

2. Trying to "make" the person become a Christian by being pushy, tricky, or impatient.

3. Carrying a Bible without any positive plan for using it.

Good Witnessing Techniques
1. Sharing your life-style with others (assuming that your life-style does reflect Jesus Christ).

2. Building a friendship with another person so that person can see Christ at work in your life; meeting people where their needs are.

3. Sharing tracts and Scripture with a positive, personal touch.

4. Really listening to others as well as talking to them.

As you close your session, give kids a few minutes of silence to think about who God might want them to witness to. Let volunteers commit themselves to share their testimony with someone this week. Then pray that God will help kids have the right words to say as they attempt to tell others about Him.

REALLY READY

Session Aim

That your students will not be shaken by hostile responses to the Gospel message.

Key Verse

"I have come into the world as a light, so that no one who believes in me should stay in darkness" (John 12:46).

Things You'll Need

- Bibles
- Pencils
- Paper
- "Reactions Galore" (Action Sheet 9A)
- "Reaction Role plays" (Action Sheet 9B)

Many kids expect negative responses when they try to serve by witnessing to their friends. But few know how to handle those negative responses well. And non-Christians' responses to Christ may be greatly influenced by the Christian's handling of their questions. So it's important that we be as well-prepared as possible to help others fully understand what Christ is offering to them.

Use this session to study how Jesus handled difficult responses to His message, and to help your kids learn to handle tough responses themselves.

1

HANDLING THE TOUGH STUFF

Goal: That your students will tell how they might feel if they received hostile responses to their witness.

When you think something's great, you talk about it a lot. Your favorite TV show, maybe. Or a favorite sports player. It gives you a warm feeling inside when people agree with you. Then you grin and talk more!

But how about when kids disagree with you—or are even downright nasty? Makes you feel lousy.

Suppose for a minute that we're all just as excited about telling people about Christ as about our favorite TV show. I am going to give you some reactions of non-Christians to the Gospel. You tell how you think you might feel and maybe react if people really acted this way.

Read each response below and let a couple of kids say how they would react.

- You witness and the person says, "Wow. That's just the message I need. I'm ready to accept Christ right now."

- You witness to a kid at school who laughs and begins to make fun of you in a loud voice. A small crowd starts to gather.

- You bring along a Bible storybook to read to the children on your baby-sitting job. The mother sees the book and says, "Don't you dare read those fairy tales to my kids."

- You are passed over for a job at the grocery store because you told the man why you didn't want to work Sundays. He says that he respects you, but he thinks he would get along better with a kid who wasn't so "religious."

- You share Christ with a neighbor. He says, "That's great for kids, but you'll get over it when you're older."

- You share how you feel about Christ with your non-Christian parent, and he or she says, "I'd be more willing to listen to your God talk if you did a little more around here to help out."

We get some good responses, and often bad ones, when we follow Christ's command to tell others about Him. So do we have a perfect right to shut up? No! Jesus Himself faced many different types of responses to His message. Some were good and some were bad. He kept right on doing and saying what He knew His Father wanted. That's our assignment, too. We are to keep on sharing our message no matter how others respond.

2 REACTIONS GALORE!

Goal: That your students will list and discuss the kinds of reactions Christ got to His message of salvation.

To start off this section of your session, give your kids the following information in a mini-lecture.

The atmosphere in Jerusalem that last week of Jesus' life on earth was as explosive as dynamite.

Every year at Passover time, thousands of visiting Jews flocked into the city. The Romans knew this could mean trouble, and they prepared for it by bringing extra troops into Jerusalem. They knew the Jews hated them, and, even though Israel had been conquered by the Romans along with all of the known world, this small nation refused to buckle down and act conquered!

Small bands of Jews were always arising to challenge the Romans' power. No doubt those Romans who knew about Jesus wondered if He, too, planned to lead a rebellion against them.

Jesus was on His way to Jerusalem, but not for the reasons the Jewish people hoped and the Roman people feared.

During Jesus' time, the Law required every male Jew who was at least 12 years old and who lived within 15 miles of Jerusalem to celebrate Passover in the city. And every Jewish man all over the land wanted to attend Passover in Jerusalem at least once in his lifetime.

That year as in all other years when half a million people crowded into the Holy City, the city was prepared. Roads were repaired, bridges strengthened, and houses cleaned.

Jesus was ready, too. His journey into Jerusalem was no sudden decision. He had planned it well in advance, and had sent His disciples ahead to find the donkey He would ride.

For Jesus as well as for the Romans, the city was explosive. The Pharisees were ready to kill Him because He threatened their authority. And the people were ready to crown Him King as long as they thought He was the Messiah they wrongly believed would overthrow the Romans.

When Jesus rode into Jerusalem, thousands of people received Him like a king. The people spread their garments on the ground before Him and waved palm branches (the sign of royal triumph). They cheered and called Him "King of Israel."

Yet Jesus rode into Jerusalem on a donkey! The Pharisees must have jeered and shouted, "He's an imposter! A real king would ride in on a war-horse, not on a donkey!"

But Jesus didn't come as the great warrior king the Jews had long dreamed of; He came as the Prince of Peace. The people didn't understand.

Jesus told them He had to die so He could bring life. But the crowd couldn't understand this either. They had always thought the Messiah would live on earth and rule here forever.

Misunderstanding, disappointment, jealousy, hate—the people at the prodding of the chief priests and Pharisees were about to set off an explosion that will be heard in every nation as long as the world lasts.

Now pass out copies of "Reactions Galore!" (Action Sheet 9A). Most students enjoy working in small groups, so you may want to divide your kids into pairs or teams. But if your class enjoys working all together or working as individuals and sharing later, structure the study that way.

The study is printed for you here with answers similar to those your kids might give.

Reactions Galore!

1. Read John 12:12, 13, 19-22. Study the references listed in order to complete the chart below.

2. Now put a star beside the reaction you think pleased Jesus most. Be ready to tell why.

The answer to the "why" portion of this question is most important. "The disciples" is the obvious answer, but some students might think it took more work for the Greeks to come. Perhaps Jesus was most pleased with them.

3. Put a line through the reaction you think hurt Jesus most. Be ready to tell why.

Again, the "why" is important. The obvious answer is "the Pharisees," but perhaps the crowd could be another answer. They misunderstood Jesus, and they would turn on Him so quickly. He knew this, and their turning may have been more difficult to take than the constant hate of the leaders.

4. Just what was Jesus' message? Explain in words a fourth grader would understand what Jesus was telling people about Himself in John 12:23, 32.

(Basically Jesus' message was one of conversion—turning from sin to

People Who Heard Jesus' Message	People's Reactions to Jesus' Message
a. Crowd	a. Seemed happy. We know that they misunderstood.
b. Pharisees	b. Hated message, jealous.
c. Greeks	c. Interested enough to ask. Maybe shy. Went through disciples.
d. Disciples	d. Gave lives for Jesus— learning more about message.

Him. This represents a change in leadership in our lives, attitudes, and actions. Jesus' message was a lifesaving one, but it was not an easy one.)

5. Jesus draws an important word picture of Himself in John 12:35, 44-46. Study that picture, and use words, symbols, and stick figures to draw the message Jesus was giving those who were willing to hear.

Have kids complete their drawings and then explain them to the class.

3 REACTION READY

Goal: That your students will role play difficult situations in witnessing.

We've seen throughout this session that people have responded to Jesus in different ways. But a negative response never made Him afraid to continue telling His message.

We, too, will meet with positive and negative responses when we tell others about Christ. We should be prepared for these various responses and never let a negative one stop us from continuing to share our salvation truth with others.

Have your kids perform the following role plays.

Read the first situation from "Reaction Role Plays" (Action Sheet 9B) to your group. Then show only the student playing the non-Christian the reaction to that situation. He or she should try to act the way the printed reaction suggests.

After each role play is completed, have kids discuss what was good about the way the Christian handled the situation. Encourage them to offer suggestions about additional things the Christian could have done or said to present Christ.

The situations are printed for you here:

Reaction Role Plays
Situation 1
You, a Christian, are inviting a non-Christian to church. Don't be surprised if he or she is not too thrilled with the idea. See if you can figure out a way to overcome the person's negative responses without turning him or her off.

Reaction: Be hesitant. For years you have believed that church is just for out-of-it adults. Make your decision on whether you will come by the way the Christian handles your reaction.

Situation 2
You, a Christian, have a non-Christian family. You are talking with your older sister about Christ. Try to handle your sister's negative responses as well as you can.

Reaction: You are skeptical. You know your little brother (or sister) isn't perfect, and you always thought Christians were. Decide whether or not to become a Christian by the way your brother or sister handles your reaction and questions.

Close your session by having kids pray sentence prayers asking God to give them opportunities to witness this week. Ask that kids will have wisdom to handle both positive and negative reactions to their witness in ways that would be pleasing to God.

SESSION 10 # SERVANT GREATNESS

Session Aim

That your students will discover how Christ's view of greatness contrasts with the world's, and that they will begin to adopt His view.

Key Verse

"Whoever wants to become great among you must be your servant, and whoever wants to be first must be slave of all" (Mark 10:43b, 44.)

Things You'll Need

- *Bibles*
- *Pencils*
- *Paper*
- *Chalkboard and chalk*
- *"That's Honor?" (Action Sheet 10A)*
- *"Attitude Aptitudes" (Action Sheet 10B)*

Who are the winners in this world? *The statesmen, the sports stars, the money-makers, the dynamic speakers? We're used to judging greatness according to talent, skill, looks, wisdom, confidence—even according to Bible knowledge and the ability to use "spiritual" jargon.*

Some of these qualities are fine, but none of them qualifies a person for greatness in Jesus' eyes. Our Lord measures greatness according to how much we serve.

Jesus didn't talk about service in the same way that a politician talks about "serving" a constituency. Christ instructed His followers to do even menial things for others, without concern for reward. And it's not just the actions that are important; Jesus sees the attitudes, too.

Use this session to help your kids develop servants' hearts, with Jesus as their example. Give them the opportunity to be great by God's standards.

1 TRULY GREAT

Goal: That your students will describe the qualities of a great person.

Have you ever heard people say of a person, "There goes a great man (or woman)!" The dictionary defines a great person as someone who's grand, distinguished, or "markedly superior in character."

Think of someone you know who you think is truly great.

What qualities make a person truly great?

Have kids brainstorm a list of qualities of greatness. Make the list as long as possible. Add your own ideas to these starter ideas:

A truly great person
- *is generous*
- *really listens—genuinely concerned about others*
- *has lots of insight, wisdom*
- *is never pushy, though can be forceful*
- *is strong*
- *does not brag.*

If you have time, ask kids to also make a list describing the opposite of greatness. Then take a poll:

How many of you would like to be great someday? In today's session, Jesus tells us how to become the greatest of the greats.

2 A NEW IDEA

Goal: That your students will develop mini-dramas based on Scripture passages that demonstrate Christ's teaching on true greatness.

We're going to examine three different situations in which Jesus taught His disciples about being truly great. And we're going to use drama to do it.

Pick students to read the roles of Andrew, Matthew, Peter, and Jesus. Distribute copies of "That's Honor?" (Action Sheet 10A). The script on the sheet is a dramatization of Mark 10:35-45. Have your students read through the script, putting as much life into it as possible.

The script is printed for you here:

That's Honor?

by Pete Herr

Andrew: Matthew, did you hear what James and John just asked Jesus? They want the places of honor in His Kingdom!

Matthew: Yeah, I heard them. Who do they think they are, anyway?

Andrew: Beats me. I can think of plenty of people who are a lot more deserving than those two. It's easy to see how they got their nickname— Sons of Thunder! They're all just noise and no clout.

Matthew: I hope Jesus really puts them in their place. It would be good for them. They've got no right trying to set themselves above the rest of us.

Andrew: Well, maybe we shouldn't depend on Jesus to put them in their place, especially since He's so loving all the time. Here comes my brother, Peter. He'll speak up to Jesus anytime. Let's talk to him and then we can all go together to demand our rights.

Matthew: Hey, Peter. James and John have asked Jesus for the honor of sitting by His right hand and by His left hand when He establishes His Kingdom.

Peter: Those conniving scoundrels! They aren't going to get away with this. C'mon, let's go see Jesus and put a stop to this scheme.

Andrew: Now hold on, Pete. We have to plan exactly what you are going to say so that Jesus will have to be fair with us.

Peter: Well, okay. Give me your ideas.

Phillip: Maybe the first thing is to discredit James and John. Mention some of the stupid things they have done. And since Jesus is always concerned about the type of persons we are, let's cast some doubt on their whole character. After you've done that, Peter, then you've got to tell how great we are. Look at everything we gave up. Look at all the hardships we've endured. Look at how faithful we've been. He's got to see that it's only fair that we all be treated alike.

Peter: Okay, this should give me all the ammunition I need. Jesus is down by the well. Let's go talk to Him.

Peter: Teacher, we heard about James and John asking You for the places of honor in Your Kingdom. We want to talk to You about it.

Jesus: Why don't all of you gather around Me and listen closely? As you know, the kings and great men of the earth lord it over the people; but among you it is different. Whoever wants to be great among you must be your servant. And whoever wants to be greatest of all must be the slave of all. For even I am not here to be served, but to help others, and to give My life as a ransom for many.

Peter: I'm really not sure I understand everything You are saying, but suddenly it doesn't seem like the positions of honor are all that important.

After kids have presented the dramatic reading, you may want to elaborate on this story by sharing the following information:

James and John appear as villains in this story, until we ask ourselves why the other apostles were so upset. The answer is simple. They wanted those same chief seats themselves.

Customs in Jesus' day dictated certain places of honor. In a king's throne room, it was considered most honorable to be at the immediate right or left side of the throne. A king's top advisers would be there, close at hand. James and John wanted to be closest to their Master in the places of honor.

In Jesus' day, a display of many servants, with long procession going before the ruler and a long train following after, was the mark of an important man.

Jesus pointed out a new idea: he is greatest who serves most. The goal is not to be served but to serve. And Jesus used the strong word, "slave." He commanded His followers—and that includes us—to be slaves of others. We are not forced into it at dagger point. Our service is not a drudgery, but the gift of love.

Jesus knew that His disciples didn't see that true greatness could be found only in serving others. He would give them the greatest example of this when He served the world by going to the cross to die for the world's sin.

Now divide your group into groups of three or four. Assign Matthew 22:35—23:12 to half of the groups, and assign Matthew 18:1-6; Mark 9:33-37; and Luke 9:46-48 to the other half of the groups. Give each group passages, and ask them to develop their own mini-dramas, much like the one you just read through.

To make the Scriptures into plays, kids will have to decide what each character might have said. Challenge kids to keep the meaning of the story the same and to stick as closely as possible to the words Jesus actually said.

After kids have prepared, have them share their plays with the rest of your group. Then discuss the questions listed below. (Note: This study may take longer than usual, so plan on plenty of time for this activity. If you are short on time, just read through the Scripture passages and discuss the questions.)

Mini-drama I: Matthew 22:35—23:12. What are some of the things the Pharisees should have been doing if they had really been following God's principles?

(Helping people with problems and giving the places of honor to others.)

What things might a modern "Pharisee" do that would be just as non-Christian as the things the Pharisees in Jesus' day did?

Mini-drama II: Matthew 18:1-6; Mark 9:33-37; Luke 9:46-48. Why do you think the disciples were finding this lesson in serving so difficult?

State the message of this mini-drama in a single sentence.

A question for both groups:

According to Jesus, what's the surest way to achieve greatness?

(Through service.)

Do you agree? Think back to the beginning of the lesson and how you described the person you said was great.

Let kids discuss. Try to be aware of any problems they might be having with the concept of greatness as service.

Then read today's Key Verses to your kids:

"Whoever wants to become great among you must be your servant, and whoever wants to be first must be slave of all" (Mark 10:43b, 44).

Have kids discuss what Jesus said, then wrap up this section by paraphrasing the following paragraphs.

Jesus not only taught His disciples to be servants, He showed them how by His life and His example. He was God, yet He showed His greatness by being a servant. He wasn't afraid to practice what He preached.

Christ's example was not only for His disciples who walked with Him on earth, but also for us, His disciples today.

He expects the attitudes of a servant to be found in us—attitudes of humility, unselfishness, putting others first, concern, compassion, and genuine love.

He expects these attitudes to be expressed in our actions, through deeds of thoughtfulness and kindness to others.

3 A GREAT ATTITUDE

Goal: That your students will take a self-test to help them measure their attitudes in relation to Biblical greatness.

Of course, it would be possible to be involved in many service activities without having the right attitudes. Since real greatness is an inner quality, it's hard to see. But let's take a quiz that can help us check our inner attitudes.

Hand out copies of "Attitude Aptitudes" (Action Sheet 10B). Explain that kids are to read each statement and then write "Great!" on their papers if that statement is true of them. If they know the statement is not true of them, they should write "small."

The quiz is printed for you here.

Attitude Aptitudes

1. I don't have to be the center of attention all the time.
2. I am willing to really listen when others talk.
3. My conversation is not filled with talk about myself.
4. I don't brag about myself or my successes.
5. I don't have to have the best of everything in order to be happy.
6. It doesn't bother me when I don't always get credit for things I do or ideas I have.
7. People often come to me and ask me to do favors for them.
8. I am willing to help others even if I know they will never help me in return.
9. I seriously pray for others as much or more than I pray for myself and things I want.
10. I work hard at all the tasks I accept.
11. I never ask other people to do things that I wouldn't be willing to do myself.
12. I am happy when other people succeed even if it means they are doing better than I am.

Give kids time to think silently about their evaluations.

This coming week, why not pray that God will help you get rid of the small attitudes in your life—the areas where you are proud or unwilling to serve Him. Ask Him to make you willing to be a truly great person—a servant.

Suggest that kids spend the last few minutes of your session silently asking God to help them be the types of servants He can use. Close with your own prayer for all of you.

HARD LOVE

Session Aim

That your students will respond to the needs of even the most "undesirable" people with respect and concern.

Key Verse

"Say of your brothers, 'My people,' and of your sisters, 'My loved one'" (Hosea 2:1).

Things You'll Need

- *Bibles*
- *Pencils*
- *Paper*
- *"Totaled Toe" (Action Sheet 11A)*
- *"Not the Usual Love Story" (Action Sheet 11B)*
- *Poster board*
- *Markers*

You've probably seen them: the unshaven, disheveled transient on a city street; the woman in dirty clothes that were fashionable ten years ago; rowdy kids who throw beer bottles on your lawn as they speed through your neighborhood. *These are undesirable people—people who are hard to love.*

There are undesirable people in your kids' schools, too. Some may be rejected simply because they don't wear the right clothes. Some may not be very clean, and may not smell the best. They may not seem to "deserve" love.

But do we deserve God's love? Fortunately for us, there are no "rejects" in His eyes. Use this session to help your kids learn to love those "undesirables" as Christ loves us.

1 TOTALLY REJECTED TOE

Goal: That your students will demonstrate reactions they often have to those who are undesirable.

Before class, cut apart the slips on "Totaled Toe" (Action Sheet 11A). When kids arrive, give one slip to each. If you have more than 5 kids, break them into groups and give one slip to each group. Give them these general directions:

A big toe has come to you for help. It says that no one loves it because it's so ugly. People take one look and giggle, whisper, or totally reject it. It asks you how you feel about it, and then it goes away to give you time to talk about it. Follow the special directions on your slip. Be ready to tell what you came up with.

Here are the directions from the slips:

Totaled Toe
1. Decide ways to be rather nice to Toe.
2. Think about reasons to reject Toe.
3. Decide on ways to avoid Toe.
4. Talk about reasons to completely accept Toe.
5. Make jokes about Toe.

After kids have shared, discuss the following questions:

What kinds of people might the toes have represented?

What kind of people did you represent?

Our reactions to ugly toes can be funny, but when we have poor reactions toward people it's not funny anymore. What kinds of things make people undesirable to us?

God expects us to accept all people who follow Christ into our circle of friends. But He takes it a step farther. God expects us to care about others who may be downright undesirable and nasty.

2 A STORY OF LOVE

Goal: That your students will discuss how Hosea's love story pictures God's love and our need to care for others.

Hosea is a dramatic example of what our attitude should be toward people who are unlovely. In today's Bible text, Israel and Gomer (Hosea's wife) are like the ugly toes we've just been talking about. And through Hosea's unusual life story, God was able to give Israel an important message about how He felt toward them—even when they were not loving or obedient to Him.

Pass out copies of "Not the Usual Love Story" (Action Sheet 11B). A reprint follows for your convenience. Ask kids to listen carefully as you read through the first part before they begin filling in their charts.

Not the Usual Love Story

The book of Hosea tells of an unusual love. But it's not the happy boy-meets-girl story people like to read.

Unfaithful Wife
Hosea's wife, Gomer, was unfaithful to her husband. Adultery became a habit, and she finally left the prophet Hosea and her three children.

Eventually she was abandoned by her lover and ended up in a slave market.

It's probable that she didn't become loose in her morals until after the prophet married her. But an amazing thing is that Hosea continued to love her dearly even after she left him.

God used Hosea's experiences to help Hosea describe a similar love story between Himself and Israel.

Unfaithful Israel
Hosea preached that Israel was like an unfaithful wife. She had loved God, but began to follow false gods, like Baal. She became rich and carefree, and gave false gods the credit for her joy.

Hosea warned that Israel would suffer for her spiritual adultery unless the nation came back to God.

The prophet loved his people as much as he loved Gomer, and found both tragedies equally heartbreaking. One of his children he named "Not Pitied"—God would no longer have pity on His sinful people. Another child he named "Not My People"—they had broken God's covenant.

Hosea Takes Gomer Back
Do you wonder how Hosea's personal love story ends? Well, when Gomer was on sale in the slave market, disgraced and forsaken, Hosea bought her back.

God Takes Israel Back

So what does Hosea say will happen in the love story between God and Israel? His message promised that God was willing to take unfaithful Israel back and love her.

Hosea had another child—actually born before Gomer committed adultery. This son's name was Jezreel, which means, "God sows."

His name suggests the land would be populated by Israelites—an earthly blessing that God would give them when they once again were willing to be His people.

Give kids a few minutes to review the story and complete their charts. Then have several kids report what they wrote while the rest of the students add to their lists. Here are answers kids might give:

Facts About Hosea
(Prophet
Gomer's husband
Follower of God
Kind
Forgiving
Heartbroken)

Facts About Gomer
(Hosea's wife
Adulteress
Runaway wife
Slave
Unfaithful
Mother)

What God Wanted Hosea's Story to Teach Israel
(No matter how much they were like Gomer—rejecting Him and running away from Him to idols—He would always love them and, like Hosea, make a way for them to come back to Him.)

Now involve the whole group in further discussion.

What do you like best about Hosea's love story?

Kids may express various opinions. They may choose this time to ask questions which were raised in their minds as they read about Hosea. Take the time to answer them, then return to the question above.

(Some of the things kids may like about the story are that God held out blessing for the future—Hosea's message wasn't all gloom and doom. Also, Hosea never gave up; his love for Gomer didn't die, even though she didn't deserve it at all.)

How did Hosea's experience illustrate God's forgiveness?

(Even though his wife had left him and sinned, he was willing to take her back. That is how God acted toward Israel, a nation which had turned away from God and had fallen into sin.)

How did this experience help Hosea?

(His sadness taught him how Israel's sin grieved God, and gave him a greater understanding of God's love and mercy.)

Did this experience help Israel?

Note: Some kids may feel that perhaps it didn't, in the sense that Israel didn't get the message and repent of her sin. However, as an object lesson, it was a clear picture of a truth the people had neglected and forgotten—they belonged to God and should be faithful to Him.

The situation also should have made the people see how disgusting their sin was, and how sad it made God.

Hosea was obviously being made a fool of by his faithless, sinful wife. Why do you think Hosea was willing to go through this awful experience?

(God wanted him to do this. As a prophet, Hosea wanted to do God's will and His work. God looked beyond one man's sorrow to the great lesson that Israel needed to learn.)

Be careful that your kids are not left with the impression that God deals unkindly and unmercifully with His faithful servants. Rather, He often calls them to do and say unpopular things in order to bring glory to Himself. God also provides for His people and rewards them when they endure sadness and suffering for His sake.

Do you think Hosea believed that his wife could someday straighten out and come back to him with real love?

(He probably did, especially since his message to Israel included future repentance to God and blessing from God.)

Hosea was probably helped by the hope that Gomer would come not only to him but also to God someday. He realized she was a sinner needing God, like everyone else.

Today's Scripture text is God's message of hope to His people. Let's read Hosea 2:16-23.

This passage is difficult in the King James Version. So if your kids can use newer translations, they will likely understand the passage more clearly.

After reading the passage, discuss the following questions:

What will the people's relationship to God be in the future?

(They will love Him and be faithful to Him. They will know Him as they've never known Him before.)

Why do you think God told what He would do when His people came back to Him at the same time He told about judgement?

(This was a promise of hope. This showed God's love and mercy.)

God's love is exciting! All of us, like Gomer, have sinned, but God is willing to forgive us! It doesn't matter how unlovely we've been.

If God is that accepting and forgiving of us, we should be just as accepting and loving toward others. We should treat them with respect, no matter how undesirable they are.

3 A CAMPAIGN OF CARE

Goal: That your kids will write billboard slogans to help them remember to show concern for undesirable people.

Since God is willing to accept us no matter how undesirable we are, we should follow His example and care for those we might not have considered worthy of our friendship before.

How would our world be different if all Christians really cared about other people, even those who were unlovely or undesirable?

Let kids brainstorm suggestions. Then give each student paper or posterboard and some markers.

Pretend your paper is a billboard to be placed at a busy intersection. You want the billboard's message to show Christians their responsibility to care about others, undesirable or not. What caption would you use? What simple drawings, if any?

Give kids a few minutes to work, then have them share their creations.

Now ask each student to think silently of a person he or she has considered undesirable. Suggest that kids put today's session into practice by developing a friendship with that person. To help them remember, you might have them exchange billboard idea sheets and take them home.

Close class with student prayers. Encourage kids to seek God's help in reaching out to hard-to-love people.

A LOT TO GIVE

Session Aim

That your students will give to others, particularly those who suffer physical hunger, rather than only receive.

Key Verse

"He has showed you, O man, what is good. And what does the Lord require of you? To act justly and to love mercy and to walk humbly with your God" (Micah 6:8).

Things You'll Need

- *Bibles*
- *Pencils*
- *Paper*
- *Newspaper fashion ads*
- *"Down with Greed!" (Action Sheet 12A)*
- *"A Love Gift" (Action Sheet 12B)*

Your teens may feel they've seen it all before: pictures of starving children with sad eyes and swollen abdomens, skin-and-bones mothers trying to feed newborn babies as well as two or three older children. Your kids may feel they've heard it all before: statistics about how many people go to bed hungry at night, and how many die of starvation each year.

But how real is world hunger to your class members? Have they, like so many of us, become so calloused that they don't care?

God cares about those starving people. He cares about them just as much as He cares about us. And He has made it a part of our responsibility as Christians to do what we can to help those human souls who are in desperate need. Use this session to help kids see just what it is that God requires of us, and what they can do to serve those who suffer starvation and malnutrition.

1 FASHION OVER FOOD?

Goal: That your students will begin to be concerned about hungry people in our world when they think about the things we want.

Before class, clip some large ads for fashion clothing from the newspaper. Try to get at least one for guy's and one for girl's clothes. Post them in a visible spot as students enter class. Then discuss the following questions.

How much clothing does one person need?

Do you think you have more than you need?

Would you buy some of these clothes if you had the money?

How important is fashion? Should dressing in the latest fashions be important to a Christian?

It's very easy for all of us to think that we need more things than we actually do. It's also very easy for us to ignore or become callous to the obvious and very intense needs of other people. Did you know that there are over 400 million people in the world who are permanently hungry? Many of these people will die of starvation, or die of other diseases because they are suffering from malnutrition.

It doesn't seem fair, does it? People in the world are starving, yet most of us have so much more than is necessary. And we want more.

Try to put yourself in a hungry, penniless person's place. What would you think of people like us?

Why should we as Christians be especially concerned about those who are starving?

To talk about people starving in India and Africa is pretty unreal. It doesn't seem to relate to us. It does. Maybe we're just too selfish to care.

2 GREEDY!

Goal: That your students will discuss Micah's criticism of greed, and list ways the people of his day could have used their possessions to meet the needs of others.

Greed and selfishness have always been problems. How do we use our possessions? How important are they to us? These questions have to be answered by every society and generation. Micah was a prophet sent from God to talk to His people about these very things. Let's take a look at this man.

Distribute copies of "Down with Greed!" (Action Sheet 12A). Have a student read the text above the questions, and have another student read Micah 1:1; 2:1,2.

Down with Greed!

The people of Judah had a bad case of greed. They grabbed everything in sight from anyone who was too weak or poor or scared to fight back. In fact, today's Scripture says they would lie awake nights planning wicked deeds, and then get up early so they would have time to do them.

Read the setting of today's study in Micah 1:1; 2:1, 2.

It was to these people that God called the prophet Micah. Micah was different from most of the prophets. He was successful.

Of the many prophets whose messages are recorded in the Old Testament, most appear to have been unsuccessful in their efforts to turn their kingdoms back to God.

This doesn't mean they were failures. Sometimes God sent a prophet for the sake of a small group of persons He knew would repent. Even when the people as a whole would not listen, God found a faithful few.

Now divide your group into two groups and have each work on one of the first two questions.

Learn a little more about the people God told Micah to preach to by answering these questions.

1. Look up the following passages and list the crimes Judah was guilty of: Micah 1:5, 7; 2:1, 2; 3:11; 5:12; 6:10-12.

2. In the following passages, what commands did God give against sin? Exodus 20:3, 4, 15-17; Leviticus 19:15, 35, 36; Deuteronomy 18:10.

When your kids are done, have the first group give their list of crimes. After each one is listed, ask someone from the second group to read the appropriate command that God had given about that sin, emphasizing that His people knew better. Here are how some of the sins and commands match up:

Idolatry—Exodus 20:3, 4

Stealing—Exodus 20:15, 17

Bribery—Leviticus 19:15

Witchcraft—Deuteronomy 18:10

Cheating—Leviticus 19:35, 36

Lying—Exodus 20:16

Now discuss the rest of the questions with your kids.

3. What are some crimes that Micah preached against that still bother people today?

(There many examples from the world today. Bribery is one; many politicians and officials are convicted of it. Idolatry is one, but it is not so obvious. Encourage your kids to think past the little idol that people kneel before and worship; idolatry can be anything that comes before God.

Look again at the specific sins we mentioned: cheating, lying, bribery, stealing. From whom were things being taken?

(From the poor. From those who had little.)

The people were guilty and they knew it. Micah's message made that plain. But their solution for their sins was no better than the sins themselves!

4. Read Micah 6:6, 7. What did the people want to do while having God forgive their sins?

(The people wanted to go right on being greedy and selfish, and just pay for their sin with offerings and sacrifices. They didn't really want to change—they just wanted to bribe God!)

5. Read Micah 6:8. What does Micah say a person has to do in order to have God forgive his or her sins toward Him and others?

(In order to be forgiven, the people had to change their behavior. No more selfish, greedy cheating! It required a change of heart, too. They had to stop loving their money and start loving mercy. And it meant beginning a real relationship with God.)

6. Which is easier? Why?

7. If Micah were writing to people today, how might he write verses 6 and 7? Verse 8?

Look at verse 8 again—today's Key Verse. This is the key to what God requires of people. This is all of the Law in a nutshell, so to speak. Let's read it again together:

"He has showed you, O man, what is good. And what does the Lord require of you? To act justly and to love mercy and to walk humbly with your God" (Micah 6:8).

Now read the last part of "Down with Greed."

Micah spoke to the people, telling them how God viewed their sins, explaining that God wanted them to follow Him and be fair and just in their dealings with others.

His message had little effect on King Ahaz. But Ahaz's son Hezekiah listened and spent his life trying to bring his nation to God.

Hezekiah reopened the Temple. He began again observing the Passover and destroyed idols and "high places," where people worshiped false gods.

There was constant fear in Judah that this kingdom would fall like the Northern Kingdom, but God protected the country while people followed Him. Judah lasted for more than 100 years after Israel fell.

Jeremiah says that Micah deserves at least part of the credit for the nation's extra 100 years. He stood up against people who were not serving God, told them what was what, and led them in returning to God.

3 TO GIVE OR NOT TO GIVE

Goal: That your students will decide what they will give to help lessen world hunger.

In Micah's day, the people were selfish and greedy. The cure was for them to follow God's rules, to become more concerned about others than they were about themselves. They had to learn to give to others.

Give each student a piece of paper and ask each to finish the following sentence: "To me, giving means . . ."

After kids have completed their sentences, have volunteers share what they've written.

We've talked about what giving means to us, but how far are we willing to go to rid our lives of selfishness and greed?

We need to start thinking right now of how we can start this week to be aware of world hunger. Maybe you can start a food bank at home in which you put a certain amount of money each week. You could put in the money you save not buying a hamburger or candy. Set yourself a goal to work toward.

Share your concern with your family. This would make an excellent family project.

Give your kids a few minutes to decide what they will do.

Now pass out copies of "A Love Gift" (Action Sheet 12B). Have your kids read over the sheet and think about what they will give to help hungry people. Allow time for kids to fill in what they are willing to give for fighting world hunger. Here is a copy of what the sheet contains:

A Love Gift

We can use what God gives to help meet others' needs.

God has told us what He wants us to do: "To act justly and to love mercy and to walk humbly with your God" (Micah 6:8).

Because I love God and want to follow His commands, I will give

_____

_____

to _____

to help in combating world hunger.

You might want to have some suggestions as to organizations to which your kids could give. Or you might want to handle the giving through your class or your church.

Close your session by giving opportunities for students to pray concerning their contributions toward this important world need.

THE POWER OF PREJUDICE

Session Aim

That your students will begin to serve others without favoritism.

Key Verse

"If you really keep the royal law found in Scripture, 'Love your neighbor as yourself,' you are doing right. But if you show favoritism, you sin and are convicted by the law as law-breakers" (James 2:8, 9).

Things You'll Need

- Bibles
- Pencils
- Paper
- "Reaching Out" (Action Sheet 13A)
- Chalkboard and chalk
- "Tangram Power" (Action Sheet 13B)
- Poster board or large paper
- Markers
- Old magazines

It's been over 20 years since the civil rights battles of the 1960's were waged. *Civil rights have come a long way. But there are still problems of racial prejudice around us.*

It's been almost 2,000 years since Jesus told us we should love our neighbors as ourselves, and James reminded us that we are supposed to treat everybody equally. We may have come a long way in some areas, but we still have to deal with prejudice within individuals and within the Church.

Poor, hurting people are still ignored while wealthy, influential people receive our attention. Poor, hurting teenagers are still ignored while Christian kids try to gain the approval of wealthier, popular kids. Use this session to help your kids discover the prejudice in their own lives and to begin to combat it as well as other prejudice they see.

1 SEPARATION SIMULATION

Goal: That your students will simulate an experience of rejection within the church.

As your kids enter, seat everyone wearing brown shoes (or any other obvious distinguishing characteristic that might make up a small group) separate from the rest. Put them on the floor, behind some obstacle, facing the wrong way, or in any other undesirable place apart from the main group.

Give no explanation of the seating arrangement at this time. If kids object, tell them you are conducting an experiment.

For the next couple of minutes, confine your attention to the main "in" group, ignoring the separated "out" group. If possible, bring some snack food like cookies, candy, potato chips, or doughnuts to class. Serve the food only to the in group.

Bring an interesting picture, article, or cartoon to pass around the in group and discuss with them. Make casual conversation with the in group, asking various individuals about recent school or church events.

After you've pointedly ignored the out group for a few minutes, someone in one of the groups will probably protest the unfairness. Even if they don't say so, those in the out group are probably feeling irritated about their treatment. Ask the following question of the out group.

You sound (or look) unhappy over there. What's wrong?

After their protest, bring the group together and share the refreshments with all. Then discuss the following questions.

(To out group) How did you feel while you watched us eating (or talking)?

(To in group) How many of you felt concerned that some members of the group were being left out?

(To in group) Did any of you feel uneasy about what was happening? Why didn't you say something?

This should be asked in a friendly, nonblaming way. Some may have kept silent because they did not want to challenge your leadership.

(To all) How was what just happened similar to the treatment people often receive in real life?

(For one reason or another, some people get ignored, rejected, and discriminated against by others. Prejudice against racial and ethnic minority groups leads to unfair treatment and denial of privileges and opportunities.

(People in high income brackets often don't want to associate with poor people. Those with physical handicaps also often find themselves as outcasts.)

Help your kids broaden their concept of prejudice and rejection beyond the well-publicized types, like racial prejudice. Racial prejudice is still a serious problem, but more subtle types of prejudice and snobbery influence people, too.

What do you think causes people to treat each other unkindly and unfairly?

(Often we feel that our way is right and everyone different from us is wrong or odd.)

Do you think there are people who suffer rejection and unkindness in our community? In your school? In our church?

The answer is probably "yes" to all three of these questions. Urge kids to be specific about types of people who often experience rejection.

They might mention the ethnic prejudice implicit in Polish or Jewish jokes, the snubbing or ridicule experienced by teens branded "ugly" or "funny looking." Often guys who are poor in athletics are labeled "wimps" and left out. Clothes, grades, hairstyle, speech defects, religion, and many other traits can be the basis of rejection by some groups. There are all kinds of prejudice.

2 PREJUDICED PEOPLE?

Goal: That your students will list principles from James on how God wants us to relate to others and apply these principles to two situations.

Have your kids read James 2:1-9, 14-17. After reading the Scripture, go over the following study, using the material on "Reaching Out" (Action Sheet 13A), and the questions given here.

Reaching Out

Read James 2:1-9, 14-17.

1. Who is the victim of prejudice in the church James describes?

(A poor man, probably a visitor to the church.)

2. What do you think caused this instance of discrimination?

Students should have no trouble identifying the common tendency to cater to the rich, important, and popular people while ignoring or shunning poor and unpopular individuals.

What James is saying here can be summed up in one statement: Christian character shows itself in the right treatment of others, regardless of who or what they are.

Does James say we should look down on rich people? Explain.

(No. He says that everyone, rich or poor, should be treated alike—with courtesy and love.)

What is ironic about despising the poor and catering to the rich, according to verses 6 and 7?

If necessary, explain that the wealthier class in Judea included many Sadducees, who were among the greatest opponents of Christ and the greatest persecutors of the Christians.

3. Put verse 17 into modern terms.

4. Is the person described in verses 15 and 16 showing love for his poor neighbor? Why or why not?

(He may have had a feeling of concern for this poor person, but Christian love is not feeling alone—it's action, too.)

Have your kids work in pairs on question 5.

5. Based on the Scripture you've read, write principles found there that Christians should follow in their relationships with others.

Circulate around the room and encourage kids in their research. When most of the pairs are finished, go over the principles all have found, jotting them on a chalkboard.

Here are suggested principles from the text:

1. Never treat people in different ways according to their outward appearance.

2. Don't make judgments based on evil motives.

3. Don't neglect or discriminate against poor people, because God chose the poor people of this world to be rich in faith and to possess the Kingdom.

4. Love your neighbor as yourself.

5. Faith without action is dead. Give to your brother in need.

Then discuss the following questions.

6. Which one of these principles sums up all the other ones? That is, if you had to pick out a key principle, which one do you think it would be?

Give the chalk to a volunteer to come up and circle the key principle. Most likely students will select the one which includes the statement to love our neighbor. If students lean to some other principle, respect their thinking, but through further evaluation, try to help them see that if we love our neighbor as ourself, we will fulfill all the other principles.

Suppose a friend said, "Well, I'm prejudiced against some people, but I'm not so bad. I think you and James are overemphasizing the importance of this principle." How would you respond to such a statement?

What evidence or authority would you use to support your answer? Hint: Check Matthew 5:43-48; 22:35-40; Galatians 5:14.

(Both Jesus and Paul the apostle stressed the importance of this principle of loving your neighbor. This would tend to go against the contention that James is playing it up. Jesus lists this commandment as one of the two most important commands. Paul states that the whole law is fulfilled in this commandment.)

Suppose your friend admitted you had a point, but went on to ask, "What does it mean to 'love my neighbor'?"

Let kids come up with answers. Make sure they see that the command to love our neighbors includes all those we come in contact with. You might want to mention Jesus' definition of a neighbor in the parable of the Good Samaritan (Luke 10:25-37).

Then move on to the next section of your session.

3 POSTERS AGAINST PREJUDICE

Goal: That your students will express opposition to prejudice in their own lives through the creation of posters.

Group kids into pairs and assign each pair the task of making a poster picturing their opposition to prejudice within their own lives. Be sure to keep the posters on target: Kids are not to depict opposition to prejudice they see in others, but prejudice that they see in themselves.

If you want, you can have your kids make tangram posters. Instructions for this special kind of poster are given on "Tangram Power" (Action Sheet 13B).

Encourage your kids to be creative and original in designing their posters. Provide poster board or large sheets of paper, markers, old magazines, and any other poster-making materials you have on hand.

After the completion of the posters, unveil them one at a time, letting each pair explain its poster. Discuss the posters using questions like these:

In your own life, how can you put into practice some of the ideas we've expressed here?

What can we do to lessen tensions between different groups of people and to promote kindness and mutual acceptance?

Make plans to display the kids' posters either in your classroom or in a place where other members of the church can see them. If you display them outside the room, type up an explanation of how the posters relate to what you've been studying.

Close your class with a time of silent prayer in which each person can ask for the Lord's guidance as he or she reaches out in kindness and love to others.

LAZY SYLVESTER

by Marlene D. LeFever

Sylvester was definitely the laziest workhorse on the farm. Whenever the farmer would choose Sylvester to work with another horse plowing the fields, the second horse would groan, "Oh, no! This means I'll be stuck with double duty because Sylvester never pulls his weight."

It hadn't always been this way. The older horses remembered when Sylvester first came to the farm. The farmer was so proud of his purchase and explained to the other horses that Sylvester would be a team horse.

The young horse was warmly welcomed. After all, another horse meant they would not have to work quite as hard.

During his training period, Sylvester worked so hard he would come back to the stall in the evening in a lather. His partner horse would praise him for walking in step with him so the weight of the plow would be evenly pulled. The farmer complimented him for always looking straight ahead so the plowed rows were beautifully straight. In those days Sylvester never balked, or stopped in the middle of a row to nibble daisies.

Sylvester remembered the day when he started to change. He awakened with stomachache. "I wish I hadn't eaten so many oats last night," he moaned. "I feel like I swallowed the barn."

His fellow horses sympathized. "Maybe you won't be chosen to work today."

But he was. That morning, for the first time, Sylvester didn't pull his weight. Hiram Horse, his partner, didn't say anything about the extra work he was forced to do.

By the middle of the morning, Sylvester's stomach didn't hurt any longer, and he could have been a lot more help. But it was great not to be hard at work. "After all," he told himself, "everyone needs a vacation. I'm sure the farmer would agree."

From that time on, Sylvester took every opportunity to do less than his share. Any excuse—a bruised foot, an old horseshoe, a gnat bite on his ear—was enough to make him shirk his duty until only the oldest horses could remember the days when Sylvester was an asset to the farm crew.

Then one day the farmer sat down on a pile of straw near Sylvester and looked sadly at him. "You're useless to me," he said. "Unless you work harder, I'll have to change my plans for you."

Sylvester was shocked. Until now, he wasn't sure the farmer had even noticed his sloppy work. And he figured if the farmer did notice, he wouldn't care much. How important is one horse?

So for a few weeks, Sylvester worked like a horse. His back ached and his legs were weary. "It's not worth the pain," he thought one day. And he slacked off just a bit. The next day he did a little less, and finally, he slipped back into his sloppy habits.

When the farmer brought a new horse into the barn several months later, all the horses were excited. Sylvester rushed out with all of them to welcome the newcomer. But before he finished neighing his *hello*, the farmer said, "He'll be using your stall, Sylvester. I'm putting you out to pasture."

Sylvester's nose turned an embarrassed red. He didn't even turn to say good-bye to his fellow workers, and none of them trotted after him to say they were sorry to see him go.

After he got over his humiliation, Sylvester began to like the pasture. It was great to run free in the field, and for days he alternated between eating fresh grass and running from one fence to the other.

"I'm having a wonderful time," he told himself many times a day. But finally he had to admit that he was bored with eating and running. His life didn't have a purpose any longer. He tried to keep himself from looking at the horses working in the fields. They made him feel more useless.

"If only I had another chance to show the farmer I've changed," he thought. "I would make him so proud of me."

THE TALENT TALE

Today when we say a person has talents, we mean he has abilities. But in Jesus' day, a person with lots of talents was rich. A talent was a large amount of money—equal to the total wages of a Jewish working man for almost 20 years. A talent was a fortune!

Even though the talents in the story we're going to look at today were money, Jesus wanted His listeners to apply the parable to much more than money. He wanted them to understand that talents were also abilities given to them by God. In fact, our English word talent, *meaning ability, comes from this parable.*

Jesus told the Parable of the Talents to His followers on the Mount of Olives just a few days before His crucifixion. He knew He would soon leave His disciples and he wanted them to be like the five-talent man and the two-talent man. He wanted them to make good use of their abilities to serve Him and draw more people into the Kingdom of God.

1. Now read the parable in Matthew 25:14-30. When you're finished, correct the three false statements below.

   A. The five-talent man got praised because he had so many talents to begin with.

   B. The poor one-talent man didn't have a chance. He was set up to be a loser.

   C. This parable teaches that the rich get richer and the talented automatically get more talented.

2. If you just read verse 29, you could really get mixed up about what the Bible was teaching. But you have to read the Bible in chunks. One verse builds on the next; the whole thing fits together. Based on the whole parable, what does verse 29 mean?

3. One more false statement to refute: Not all Christians have talents.

TRIAL TASKS

Task A

Without bothering any other group or class, find a hymnal or a songbook outside of this room, and bring it back.

Task B

Without bothering any other group or class, find a church bulletin outside of this room, and bring it back.

Task C

Without bothering any other group or class, find a Bible with a black cover outside of this room, and bring it back.

Task D

Without bothering any other group or class, get a cup, fill it half full of water, and bring it back to this room.

CALLED TO SERVE

God used different ways of communication with His prophets, but all of them got the message and responded.

Assignment One:
The Call of Isaiah

Read Isaiah 6:1-11 and answer the following questions.

1. Suppose you had never before heard of God. What would you know about Him after reading this passage?

2. In what ways does Isaiah respond to God during this confrontation?

3. What instructions and preparation is Isaiah given for the work he will do?

Assignment Two:
The Call of Amos

Read Amos 7:10-17 and answer the following questions.

1. Suppose you had never before heard of God. What would you know about Him after reading this passage?

2. Put yourself in Amos's place at the time of his call. What doubts and fears do you have about the work God has given you? What makes you agree to serve?

3. What evidence does this passage provide of Amos's faith and courage?

Assignment Three:
The Call of Jeremiah

Read Jeremiah 1:4-19 and answer the following questions.

1. Suppose you had never before heard of God. What would you know about Him after reading this passage?

2. What assurance does this chapter provide for those called by God?

3. Put yourself in Jeremiah's place. How might you feel about delivering this message?

Our specific calls come when we commit ourselves to Christ. Jesus said, "If anyone would come after me, he must deny himself and take up his cross daily and follow me" (Luke 9:23). What this means is that when we commit ourselves to Him, He calls us to serve Him in whatever way we can.

In some cases God gives a person a special call as He did in the days of the prophets. These people know at a specific time and place what God is calling them to do, and they carry an extra responsibility with them.

No matter what we are called to do, either now or in the future, our lives should show the characteristics of a person who has accepted Christ's call to serve.

THE CONTEST

Part I

Just as Elijah had prophesied, Israel was suffering through years of drought and famine. King Ahab and Queen Jezebel, in retaliation, had ordered the death of Elijah, but Elijah had escaped. They did not recognize that it was their own wickedness that had brought about the dry skies and barren fields.

One day, at the end of three years, Elijah sent a message for Ahab to meet him.

"You troublemaker!" Ahab said as Elijah greeted him.

"Don't blame me, Ahab, you're the one who worships Baal and ignores God's commandments."

Before the king could get a word in, Elijah went on. "If you want to settle this," he said, "have all the people meet me at Mount Carmel. Be sure that the 450 prophets of Baal are there."

Ahab agreed.

To find out what happened, read I Kings 18:20-40.

Part II

After the contest was over, Elijah killed all the prophets of Baal to make it harder for the people to revert to idol worship. God had demonstrated that He was in control.

Because Elijah had the courage to fight against evil, the Israelites—except for the wicked king and queen—were once more ready to repent and follow God.

Part III

1. Why do you think all the water was poured on the sacrifice and in the trench?

3. Why do you think Elijah had the prophets of Baal killed? What principle for dealing with evil can we see in this?

2. What do you think the fire sent from Heaven proved?

DECISIONS, DECISIONS!

Sometimes seeing what is right is easy, but doing it is hard. Other times it's hard to even see what is the right thing to do. Take a look at these fictitious characters and discuss what they did right and wrong.

Frederick Holmes ran a small store in rural Kentucky during the 1850s. When business was light he often read his Bible. After much prayer, he became sure that slavery was not right in the eyes of God. Yet many of his customers were slave owners. He began to talk to them about their sin. They scoffed. One night he heard a knock on his door. It was a black man, a runaway slave. Frederick Holmes knew it was not legal to hide runaway slaves, but he took the slave in. Soon others arrived, and Holmes did his best to get them to freedom, breaking the law time after time.

Mary Stephenson is a one-woman crusade against pornography. She has picketed bookstores and tried to talk to high school teachers who she thought were assigning reading from "dirty" books. She attends every city council meeting and started asking if she could address them on "the filth that is rampant in our city." One day they agreed to hear her out. She talked for 45 minutes and held up several examples of magazines that she felt should not be allowed to be displayed and sold in the city. When the mayor told her that the kind of ordinance she wanted was unconstitutional, she shouted that the Constitution should be changed if that was true.

Juan Venido is a low-level clerk in a major federal agency. About a year after he got his job, his boss asked him to "take care" of some money for him. At first Juan did what he was told, but when more and more money kept coming in, he got suspicious. It looked like something illegal was going on. One day he overheard a conversation that confirmed his suspicions. The next time his boss asked him to "take care" of some money, he refused. Later he learned that another clerk was doing it. Juan felt he should tell someone, but was afraid he'd lose his job. So instead of going to the police, he merely gave a "tip" to a newspaper reporter he knew. That night he prayed that someone would find out what was happening and put a stop to it.

KINDNESS COUNTS

Susan

Susan is walking around in a crowded mall. Suddenly she spots Amanda, a girl in her class at school. Amanda hasn't seen Susan. Amanda is the leech type, but she looks lonely. Susan debates whether to go over and risk having Amanda follow her around the mall. She's just about decided to go over there when Amanda starts to turn in Susan's direction. Susan slips quickly around the corner, out of sight, and says to herself, "Aw, it doesn't matter anyway."

Jeff

Jeff is home alone reading a book. It's nearly lunchtime, and he's about to go downstairs to fix a sandwich when the doorbell rings. Looking out the window of his second-story bedroom, he sees Mrs. Adleman standing on the front porch. He remembers hearing his mom say that Mrs. Adleman was going to stop over sometime collecting for the mission hospital project. Mrs. Adleman doesn't see Jeff at the window above.

Jeff debates: If he answers the door, he'll have to give out of his own pocket. Mrs. Adleman will probably come back when his folks are home, anyway. But he could save her the trip by giving now. He just got his allowance and hasn't given any of it to God yet. Jeff is still debating when Mrs. Adleman turns to walk away. Jeff shrugs and says to himself, "Well, it doesn't matter anyway," and heads downstairs to the kitchen.

Lynn

Lynn is hanging around the hall near the phone booth after school with some of her friends. A woman rushes in and enters the phone booth. She searches her purse, then opens the door and says, "Do any of you kids have change for a dollar?"

Lynn knows that she does, but for some reason she just stands there. She had saved that change in case she wanted a candy bar on her way home from school. Mary, a friend, searches through her purse, but can only find 75 cents. Lynn is just about to reach for her purse when the woman says to Mary, "Well, here's the dollar, I'll take your 75 cents." Lynn sighs and says, "Oh, well. She got what she needed for the phone. It doesn't matter."

A Very Important Animal Story

1. Read today's text and write down all the things you have learned about the people called sheep in this parable.

2. Read Matthew 25:31-33, 41-46 and write down things you have learned about the people called goats in this parable.

Those sheep were really busy doing things for others. Jesus mentions six good deeds the sheep did. These good deeds stand for any service done in Christ's name, not just the six things mentioned.

3. These good deeds have some things in common. Name at least two of them.

4. What might be two other examples of the kind of good deeds the sheep do?

Jesus is not saying that we can earn eternal life and become part of His family by doing good deeds. He is saying that when we serve others and lovingly give to them as part of our Christian service to Him, we are proving that we love Him.

5. What word in verse 34 shows that we don't earn eternal life?

People who aren't Christians do nice things, too, but these things aren't done for Jesus. Non-Christians don't belong to Him; they are still goats—often nice goats, but totally separated from God no matter how good they seem. Only as we admit our sin can we receive Christ's complete forgiveness.

6. Why were the goats surprised at their sentence?

If you are a sheep (Christian), God can actually use the service you do in the name of Christ as a way to turn goats (non-Christians) into sheep—to help non-Christians find Christ as Savior.

DOUBLE DILEMMAS

Anne's Dilemma

Margo's parents are separated, and her father lives 2,000 miles away. After a serious fight with her mother, Margo is ordered out of the house at 11:30 p.m. Not knowing where to go for help, she goes to a phone booth near her house and calls Anne, one of her classmates at school. To complicate things, Anne is planning to leave at 7:00 in the morning to go shopping with a couple of close friends. One girl's mother is planning to take them in their four-seat car.

Role-play Anne and Margo completing the phone conversation in the way you think you would respond in that situation.

Ted's Dilemma

Mike's parents are separated, and his father lives 2,000 miles away. After a serious fight with his mother, Mike is ordered out of the house at 11:30 p.m. Not knowing where to go for help, He goes to a phone booth near his house and calls Ted, one of his classmates at school. To complicate things, Ted is planning to leave at 7:00 in the morning to go to a college football game with a couple of close friends. One guy's dad is planning to take them in their four-seat car.

Role-play Ted and Mike completing the phone conversation in the way you think you would respond in that situation.

PAPER CLIPS AND LOVE

1. Overpopulation, famine, disease, and crime are everywhere. What is a Christian supposed to do in the face of all these pressing needs?

2. Read Matthew 9:35-38. Take your first paper clip and twist it into a sculpture illustrating one quality Jesus showed toward others in this passage.

3. Consider what Christ did as He traveled through the cities and villages of His land. List persons or groups of persons who are doing some of these same things in our day.

4. Read Matthew 10:1, 7, 8. In verses 7 and 8, the Lord directed the disciples to be active in five areas as they contacted people. List each area.

5. Take a close look at these five areas and then summarize what must have been Jesus' idea of evangelism. (Hint: How does Jesus relate physical needs to spiritual needs?)

6. Read I John 3:16-18. Take your second paper clip and illustrate one important principle Christians should find in this passage.

7. Most people have not had the opportunity to lay down their lives for others. However, God has defined this sacrifice of laying down one's life in a practical way that every Christian has the opportunity to carry out. According to verse 17, what is a practical way one's life can be laid down for others?

8. True love is more than a warm feeling. What yardstick does God use when He evaluates our love?

9. Now take your last paper clip and illustrate one of the ways you could put love into action.

SERVANT SAVIOR

Read John 13:3-15, and then answer the following questions.

1. What things can you learn about Jesus from this passage?

2. What things can you learn about the Christian life from this passage?

3. What title would you give this passage to distinguish it from all other Scripture? Write your title above the passage.

4. In what way could you apply the messages in these verses to life today?

5. Write two or three key statements about humility that you can draw from the Scripture passage below assigned to you. For example, a key statement from the passage where Jesus washed the disciples' feet might be, "Humility expresses itself in service to others." Each pair will report its findings to the group.

I Peter 5:1-6

James 4:6-10

Philippians 2:4-11

HUMILITY Is . . .

Art by Michael Streff

...HELPING THE KID NO ONE LIKES TO STRAP ON HIS SKIIS.

...ADMITTING TO YOUR LITTLE BROTHER THAT HE WAS RIGHT AND YOU WERE WRONG.

...ASKING FOR FORGIVENESS.

...ACCEPTING NURSERY DUTY AT CHURCH.

...TAKING THE TIME TO STOP BY AND VISIT SOMEONE WHO NEEDS LOVE AND ATTENTION.

OTHER PEOPLE, OTHER PLACES

There I was attending the Antioch Church when the Lord told some of the prophets and teachers who also attended there that Barnabas and I had been called for a special work. The Holy Spirit wanted us to preach in foreign lands!

Well, you can imagine what a thing like that did to my prayer life: sped it up, fast! Why, we didn't even know where to go, how to get there, or what to do once we got there! I mean, we were the first missionaries ever sent. The very first!

When we docked at Salamis, I heaved a sigh of relief. Salamis, being the most important town on the island, had a good-sized Jewish population, and was I glad to see that! Setting off for lands unknown can be mighty scary without a friendly face.

Barnabas and I headed for the synagogues (there were several in town) and preached the news about Jesus. After that we started working our way across the island. One hot, sweaty afternoon we finally made it all the way to Paphos, the capital. Things had gone well, and we were getting brave. So we decided to go see the governor of the island.

We got in to see him all right, but he had a man with him who claimed to be religious. The guy pulled off all sorts of mystical tricks.

I thought he was going to spoil everything, but God performed a miracle through me and struck him blind. You should have seen the governor (or proconsul, as he was called) sit up at that!

We sailed from there to Perga in Pamphilia. (You probably call it Turkey.) Barnabas and I started hiking through the hills to the town of Antioch (not the same Antioch we started out from). Besides, the coastal region around Perga was pretty thick with mosquitos, mostly the malaria-carrying kind.

We headed for the synagogue in this new town of Antioch and told them the story of Jesus and God's love. Well, the people said to come back next week and tell them more. So we did. Of course, we invited most of the rest of the town, too.

When the local Jews saw all those Gentiles, they were furious! Seems they wanted the Good News for themselves.

I told them that I'm a Jew, too. That's why I came to them first. But, I said, you can't expect to keep God for yourself! He's for everybody!

When I tried to speak, the Gentiles and many of the Jews rejoiced with me. However, some Jews walked out.

I could have cried. My own people! Don't they know our God is the God of the whole world?

REPORTER'S NOTEBOOK

Verse	Who?	Did What?	To or For Whom?	How?	When?	Where?	Why?
Acts 13:2							
Acts 13:3							
Acts 13:4							
Acts 13:5							
Acts 13:42							
Acts 13:43							
Acts 13:44							
Acts 13:45							
Acts 13:46							

WHAT'S IT ALL ABOUT?

ACTION SHEET 8A

by Rev. James Netters

"Pastor, what this church needs is a basketball team."

"Wrong, Jerry," I said. "This church has been broken into so often that what it needs is bars for the windows. Anyway, we don't have any boys for the team."

"You get the church to sponsor basketball," Jerry countered, "and I'll get the boys."

"What boys?"

He named them off, and each one had a court record. If they weren't the ones who had been breaking into the church on an average of twice a week, they knew who had been. Most of them had at one time or another been probated to me, pastor of the Mt. Vernon Baptist Church in Memphis, Tennessee.

I hit the ceiling. "You don't expect me to bring a bunch of thugs into church," I sputtered.

"Isn't that what the church is all about?"

A long pause. I'll never forget that pause. 16-year-old Jerry Williams had just preached the best sermon I'd ever heard, and it would change our entire church.

Our church was located across the street from a housing project. The people in our church were low-income; 95 percent of the families were fatherless. The crime rate was soaring.

I knew God was speaking to me through Jerry.

"Okay," I said. "You get the boys, and I'll take care of the other end."

I did some hard selling. We were talking about bringing the street problems into the church—through the front door instead of through the windows, the way they usually came in. The church finally bought it.

We organized big-brother programs. Each boy was directly responsible to one man for his conduct. The man, in turn, helped the teenager in every way he could.

The basketball team itself realized that if this basketball experiment was to work, each boy had to be more responsible than many of them had been before in their lives. They set up their own code of conduct. They were rough on themselves—no bad language, pick up the junk in the churchyard, no fighting, be in church every Sunday.

No fighting—and that had been a way of life! One boy got so angry at an unfair call that he lay down on the court and cried. It was the only outlet he had for his emotions when he couldn't use his fists.

We were thrilled when break-ins dropped from two a week to two a year. But the greatest reward? Within three years, all 17 of those street kids playing basketball had been baptized into the church!

Sometimes when I'm discouraged, or some job I believe God has given seems unworkable or even unreasonable, I'm reminded of the greatest sermon I've ever heard. Working for Jesus Christ, pointing those who don't love Him to God—yes, Jerry, that's what the Church is all about.

To Sow And Reap

1. To give you some background for the passage we'll study today, read John 4:6-30 and write a title describing this story.

2. Now read John 4:31-41 and write a title explaining the key message found there.

3. In explaining His message to the disciples, Jesus used some terms to symbolically communicate to them what He wanted them to learn from this situation. What did Jesus mean by His use of the following words?

a. Food

b. Fields

c. Harvest

d. The reaper

4. Explain what Jesus meant when He was talking about the reaper and the sower.

5. If Jesus had been talking to a group of city people, what symbolic illustration might He have used?

6. The Samaritans believed in Jesus for two reasons. First there was the testimony of the woman. Second, and more important, was the message of Jesus. Obviously the same is true today. People become interested in Christ and perhaps even decide to believe in Him by watching the lives of Christians and by listening to their testimonies of what Christ has meant to them.

But included in the personal testimony is Christ's message of salvation.

On a small card, write a brief outline of Christ's message of salvation as you understand it. Use Bible references wherever possible. Some you might want to use are Romans 3:23; 6:23; 10:9; John 3:16; 10:10; I John 5:11.

7. Practice sharing the message of salvation with a partner. Choose one of the situations below. Be sure to be sensitive, tell about Christ's message, and include your own personal testimony.

- A close friend of yours is in the hospital as a result of a motorcycle accident.
- A friend has come to church for the first time.
- A parent or neighbor has asked you some questions about the salvation message.

REACTIONS GALORE!

1. Read John 12:12, 13, 19-22. Study the references listed in order to complete this chart.

People Who Heard Jesus' Message	People's Reactions to Jesus' Message
a. Crowd	
b. Pharisees	
c. Greeks	
d. Disciples	

2. Now put a star beside the reaction you think pleased Jesus most. Be ready to tell why.

3. Put a line through the reaction you think hurt Jesus most. Be ready to tell why.

4. Just what was Jesus' message? Explain in words a fourth grader would understand what Jesus was telling people about Himself in John 12:23, 32.

5. Jesus draws an important word picture of Himself in John 12:35, 44-46. Study that picture, and use words, symbols, and stick figures to draw the message Jesus was giving those who were willing to hear.

REACTION ROLE PLAYS

Situation 1

You, a Christian, are inviting a non-Christian to church. Don't be surprised if he or she is not too thrilled with the idea. See if you can figure out a way to overcome the person's negative responses without turning him or her off.

Reaction: Be hesitant. For years you have believed that church is just for out-of-it adults. Make your decision on whether you will come by the way the Christian handles your reaction.

Situation 2

You, a Christian, have a non-Christian family. You are talking with your older sister about Christ. Try to handle your sister's negative responses as well as you can.

Reaction: You are skeptical. You know your little brother (or sister) isn't perfect, and you always thought Christians were. Decide whether or not to become a Christian by the way your brother or sister handles your reaction and questions.

THAT'S HONOR?

A Dramatization of
Mark 10:35-45

by Pete Herr

Andrew: Matthew, did you hear what James and John just asked Jesus? They want the places of honor in His Kingdom!

Matthew: Yeah, I heard them. Who do they think they are, anyway?

Andrew: Beats me. I can think of plenty of people who are a lot more deserving than those two. It's easy to see how they got their nickname—Sons of Thunder! They're all just noise and no clout.

Matthew: I hope Jesus really puts them in their place. It would be good for them. They've got no right trying to set themselves above the rest of us.

Andrew: Well, maybe we shouldn't depend on Jesus to put them in their place, especially since He's so loving all the time. Here comes my brother, Peter. He'll speak up to Jesus anytime. Let's talk to him and then we can all go together to demand our rights.

Matthew: Hey, Peter. James and John have asked Jesus for the honor of sitting by His right hand and by His left hand when He establishes His Kingdom.

Peter: Those conniving scoundrels! They aren't going to get away with this. C'mon, let's go see Jesus and put a stop to this scheme.

Andrew: Now hold on, Pete. We have to plan exactly what you are going to say so that Jesus will have to be fair with us.

Peter: Well, okay. Give me your ideas.

Phillip: Maybe the first thing is to discredit James and John. Mention some of the stupid things they have done. And since Jesus is always concerned about the type of persons we are, let's cast some doubt on their whole character. After you've done that, Peter, then you've got to tell how great we are. Look at everything we gave up. Look at all the hardships we've endured. Look at how faithful we've been. He's got to see that it's only fair that we all be treated alike.

Peter: Okay, this should give me all the ammunition I need. Jesus is down by the well. Let's go talk to Him.

Peter: Teacher, we heard about James and John asking You for the places of honor in Your Kingdom. We want to talk to You about it.

Jesus: Why don't all of you gather around Me and listen closely? As you know, the kings and great men of the earth lord it over the people; but among you it is different. Whoever wants to be great among you must be your servant. And whoever wants to be greatest of all must be the slave of all. For even I am not here to be served, but to help others, and to give My life as a ransom for many.

Peter: I'm really not sure I understand everything You are saying, but suddenly it doesn't seem like the positions of honor are all that important.

ATTITUDE APTITUDES

ACTION SHEET 10B

1. I don't have to be the center of attention all the time.

2. I am willing to really listen when others talk.

3. My conversation is not filled with talk about myself.

4. I don't brag about myself or my successes.

5. I don't have to have the best of everything in order to be happy.

6. It doesn't bother me when I don't always get credit for things I do or ideas I have.

7. People often come to me and ask me to do favors for them.

8. I am willing to help others even if I know they will never help me in return.

9. I seriously pray for others as much or more than I pray for myself and things I want.

10. I work hard at all the tasks I accept.

11. I never ask other people to do things that I wouldn't be willing to do myself.

12. I am happy when other people succeed even if it means they are doing better than I am.

TOTALED
TOE

1. *Decide ways to be rather nice to Toe.*

2. *Think about reasons to reject Toe.*

3. *Decide on ways to avoid Toe.*

4. *Talk about reasons to completely accept Toe.*

5. *Make jokes about Toe.*

NOT THE USUAL LOVE STORY

The Book of Hosea tells of an unusual love. But it's not the happy boy-meets-girl story people like to read.

Unfaithful Wife

Hosea's wife, Gomer, was unfaithful to her husband. Adultery became a habit, and she finally left the prophet Hosea and her three children. Eventually she was abandoned by her lover and ended up in a slave market.

It's probable that she didn't become loose in her morals until after the prophet married her. But an amazing thing is that Hosea continued to love her dearly even after she left him.

God used Hosea's experiences to help Hosea describe a similar love story between Himself and Israel.

Unfaithful Israel

Hosea preached that Israel was like an unfaithful wife. She had loved God, but began to follow false gods, like Baal. She became rich and carefree, and gave false gods the credit for her joy.

Hosea warned that Israel would suffer for her spiritual adultery unless the nation came back to God.

The prophet loved his people as much as he loved Gomer, and found both tragedies equally heartbreaking. One of his children he named "Not Pitied"—God would no longer have pity on His sinful people. Another child he named "Not My People"—they had broken God's covenant.

Hosea Takes Gomer Back

Do you wonder how Hosea's personal love story ends? Well, when Gomer was on sale in the slave market, disgraced and forsaken, Hosea bought her back.

God Takes Israel Back

So what does Hosea say will happen in the love story between God and Israel? His message promised that God was willing to take unfaithful Israel back and love her.

Hosea had another child—actually born before Gomer committed adultery. This son's name was Jezreel, which means, "God sows."

His name suggests the land would be populated by Israelites—an earthly blessing that God would give them when they once again were willing to be His people.

Facts about Hosea

Facts about Gomer

What God wanted Hosea's story to teach Israel

DOWN WITH GREED!

The people of Judah had a bad case of greed. They grabbed everything in sight from anyone who was too weak or poor or scared to fight back. In fact, today's Scripture says they would lie awake nights planning wicked deeds, and then get up early so they would have time to do them.

Read the setting of today's study in Micah 1:1; 2:1, 2.

It was to these people that God called the prophet Micah. Micah was different from most of the prophets. He was successful.

Of the many prophets whose messages are recorded in the Old Testament, most appear to have been unsuccessful in their efforts to turn their kingdoms back to God.

This doesn't mean they were failures. Sometimes God sent a prophet for the sake of a small group of persons He knew would repent. Even when the people as a whole would not listen, God found a faithful few.

Learn a little more about the people God told Micah to preach to by answering these questions:

1. Look up the following passages and list the crimes Judah was guilty of: Micah 1:5, 7; 2:1, 2; 3:11; 5:12; 6:10, 11, 12.

2. In the following passages, what commands did God give against sin? Exodus 20:3, 4, 15-17; Leviticus 19:15, 35, 36; Deuteronomy 18:10.

3. What are some crimes that Micah preached against that still bother people today?

4. Read Micah 6:6, 7. What did the people want to do while having God forgive their sins?

5. Read Micah 6:8. What does Micah say a person has to do in order to have God forgive his or her sins toward Him and others?

6. Which is easier? Why?

7. If Micah were writing to people today, how might he write verses 6 and 7? Verse 8?

Micah spoke to the people, telling them how God viewed their sins, explaining that God wanted them to follow Him and be fair and just in their dealings with others.

His message had little effect on King Ahaz. But Ahaz' son Hezekiah listened and spent his life trying to bring his nation to God.

Hezekiah reopened the Temple. He began again observing the Passover and destroyed idols and "high places," where people worshiped false gods.

There was constant fear in Judah that this kingdom would fall like the northern kingdom, but God protected the country while people followed Him. Judah lasted for more than 100 years after Israel fell.

Jeremiah says that Micah deserves at least part of the credit for the nation's extra 100 years. He stood up against people who were not serving God, told them what was what, and led them in returning to God.

A Love Gift

We can use what God gives to help meet others' needs.

God has told us what He wants us to do: "To act justly and to love mercy and to walk humbly with your God" (Micah 6:8).

Because I love God and want to follow His commands, I will give

_____

_____

to _____ to help in fighting world hunger.

REACHING OUT

Read James 2:1-9, 14-17.

1. Who is the victim of prejudice in the church James describes?

2. What do you think caused this instance of discrimination?

3. Put verse 17 into modern terms.

4. Is the person described in verses 15 and 16 showing love for his poor neighbor? Why or why not?

5. Based on the Scripture you've read, write principles found there that Christians should follow in their relationships with others.

6. Which one of these principles sums up all the other ones? That is, if you had to pick out a key principle, which one do you think it would be?

Tangram Power

A tangram (pronounced TANG-grum) is a square of any size cut in the pattern given here. Cut out the pieces of each tangram, and arrange them in a meaningful design on another sheet of paper. You might want to use a colored background paper, or you may color or overlap the pieces. The pieces may not be bent nor any more than the seven pieces be used. An example is given for you.

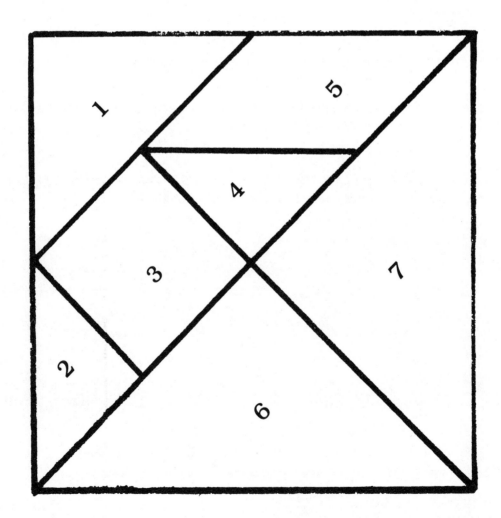